A HABIT OF SEEING

A HABIT OF SEEING

Journeys In Natural Science

Sura Jeselsohn

Full Court Press
Englewood Cliffs, New Jersey

Published in the United States of America
by Full Court Press, 601 Palisade Avenue
Englewood Cliffs, NJ 07632
fullcourtpressnj.com

ISBN 978-1-946989-30-7
Library of Congress Control No. 2019908695

Editing and book design by Barry Sheinkopf

All interior art courtesy of the author

Cover art, "Pond, Stonecrop Gardens, Carmel, New York,"
Copyright © by Barry Sheinkopf 2007

ACKNOWLEDGMENTS

I wish to acknowledge Shant Shahrigian, editor of the *Riverdale Press* in 2015, who was receptive when I approached him about writing a weekly column devoted to the natural world. Michael Hinman, the present editor (in 2019), has been a pleasure to work with.

I would also like to acknowledge the New York Botanical Garden, where I volunteered for many years. My years there fostered greater insight into the world of plants through classes and regular interaction with knowledgeable staff members.

INTRODUCTION

Many strands contributed to the genesis of this book. A particularly important one was contributed by the late Gary Lincoff, who taught an exciting introductory botany course at the New York Botanical Garden. One course requirement was a daily journal in which we were supposed to record, by date, everything that we noticed about the plants around us. While I had kept a similar journal years before, in which I noted bloom times of my garden, this journal took me further afield in that I started including entries about my extended neighborhood as well.

The natural world belongs to us all. The drive toward urbanization, however, has distanced us increasingly from this huge, complicated, and carefully balanced domain, which is not only our patrimony but which affects every aspect of our lives. Nature is not simple, and I believe we ignore it at our peril.

People have long recognized the need for greenery and the natural world. Those with private homes find solace in backyard gardens. Penthouse dwellers are creating rooftop gardens. Apartment dwellers buy houseplants and bring Nature indoors.

A good day in my book begins by checking on my plants and observing daily changes. I take this to mean that I, and my fellow botany aficionados, are acknowledging a subliminal understanding that we are part of the natural world, and we are unconsciously trying to recreate a world that is no longer familiar but whose memory has been stashed somewhere in our bones.

Horticultural Therapy's theoretical basis is that the natural world, with its varied plant life, can interact beneficently with those suffering physical illness, developmental disabilities, and/or psychological difficulties. Artificial environments may not be in our best interests.

Lena Struwe of Rutgers University spoke at a recent conference at the New York Botanical Garden. She pointed out that, in order to enjoy Nature, you do not have to travel far away to exotic parts of the world. All you need do is look around you carefully. It was exciting for me to hear someone else so clearly articulate my own thoughts.

For several years I have had the pleasure of sharing these thoughts in columns appearing in the *Riverdale Press*, which graciously gave me a platform for a weekly "Green Scene" column. I originally approached Shant Shahrigian, the editor at that time, with the idea of a column devoted to local natural history. We agreed to give it a few months and to start off slowly. When Shant left, Anna Dolgov became the new editor and was herself replaced by Michael Hinman.

I have frequently been asked how I come by my ideas. Since the paper's editors essentially give me full rein to choose topics—although sometimes the only hook to Riverdale itself is that I live here—topics almost seem to fall into my lap. Years ago I read a book on how to engage people in conversation. The only interesting tip I got was to listen carefully: Noting word choices alone can provide a chance to tease out conversational threads. I feel the same about my topics. Looking carefully, instead of just noticing what is going on around me, together with constant reading, brings more topics to my attention than I have space or time to write about.

I hope that this book will inspire more readers to do just that—not only to stop and smell the roses, but to take the time to focus on them. The natural world can be a source of endless excitement and entertainment. We just need to look around, paying close attention to what is under our noses. The rewards are enormous!

—S.J.,

Riverdale, 2019

Table of Contents

Trees and Shrubs

Insects

Birds

Animals

Potpourri

Geology

Tears of the Sun

AMBER CAN TAKE MANY FORMS, but the most beautiful suggests so-lidified honey, warm and glowing when suffused with sunlight. Several years back, I read a marvelous book, *The Amber Forest*, by George and Roberta Poinar, who used amber as a time machine to peer back into a world that vanished 45–15 million years ago. They did this by studying insect, animal, and plant inclusions encased in Dominican amber. The book lists all the plants, insects, and animal material that they found, and they concluded that the biome of that time period was a moist tropical forest that contained layered vegetation usual in such a forest—canopy, sub-canopy, and understory trees, together with a still lower-growing shrub layer and a surprisingly bare forest floor.

Raw amber has been worked into jewelry and carvings for thousands of years. Amber pieces have been found in ancient Israel, Jordan, and Mesopotamia, as well as in Tutankhamun's tomb (c. 1341–1323 BCE) in Egypt.

The puzzle presented by ancient Middle Eastern amber is that the amber originated far away in the Baltic and Scandinavian areas of northern Europe. We are familiar with the medieval Silk Road which stretched from Europe to the Far East. Apparently, there was an earlier Amber Road linking Northern Europe to the Mediterranean via the Vistula and Dnieper Rivers.

Amber has had other unusual uses. In the early 1700s, there was a 180-square-foot Amber Room in the Catherine Palace in St. Petersburg, lined with six tons of amber and other precious stones.

Numerous myths have attempted to explain the origin of amber, most involving the sun or tears. Some of the ancients, though, were already considering the idea that amber was a tree product. That conclusion may stem from its piney fragrance when burnt. In fact, the old German word for amber is *bernsten*, the source of the modern family name Bernstein where *bernen* means 'to burn' and *sten* means 'stone.'

But what *is* this semi-precious stone that is clearly so different from mineral gems? Anyone hiking through a pine forest has noticed opaque whitish blobs adhering to the bark that smell so nicely of piney fragrance. These are formed from a resin extruded by the tree, to protect itself when the bark is damaged. (Resin should not to be confused with sap, the fluid circulating inside the living tree.)

Amber is prehistoric resin that has dripped down the trunk and eventually fossilized. While the Dominican amber mentioned above can be 45 million years old, there are older ambers. Some specimens found in the United States and the United Kingdom have been dated to the Carboniferous Period, 360–285 million years ago (MYA).

Amber-like materials 2 million years or younger are not considered true amber. Although formed from resin derived from a variety of tropical trees, it represents an intermediate stage between resin and amber. Known as copal, it was used extensively by Meso-Americans as incense. By the 1800s, it had been being used by Europeans as a varnish.

In the Dominican specimens discussed earlier, the primary amber-producing tree was the extinct algarrobo, *Hymenaea protera*, which is a member of the legume family, the *Fabaceae*. Other trees suspected of producing amber can be found in the *Pinaceae* families and the *Araucariaceae*, which include the monkey-puzzle tree and the Norfolk Island pine. However, there is evidence that Baltic amber came from the family *Sciadopityaceae*, whose only surviving representative is the Japanese umbrella pine.

Amber is not my favorite gemstone, but it is a remarkable window into the past. This modality became more widely appreciated recently when Chinese scientists working in Myanmar found 99-million-year-old dinosaur segments preserved in amber. In the past, dinosaurs had generally been depicted as having scale-like skins. Recent hypotheses have suggested that, in fact, they might have been feathered. And indeed, this Myanmar specimen, containing dinosaur vertebrae, also contain two-toned feathers—brown on top and white below. These feathers do differ from contemporary bird feathers in that they do not have well developed rachis—the stiff central spine running down the center of the feather, to which the smaller structures attach. Yet, despite substantial physical differences, the specimen should help clarify feather evolution.

The prize for the oldest fossilized amber specimens goes to 230-million-year-old gall mites discovered in Italy. These creatures are arthropods from the Triassic Period—251 to 199 MYA—that feed on plants sometimes causing the formation of galls or burls which are abnormal growths on leaves, twigs, or branches. These mites are remarkably similar to today's superfamily *Eriophyoidea*, containing approximately 3,500 species.

In my opinion, amber is too entrancing to be considered anything less than tears of the sun!

The Earth Is a Dynamic Place

S TRIKE AND DIP! Strike and dip! This was the constant refrain on a pleasant autumn morning as I accompanied Dr. Howard Feldman's geology class from Touro College on a hike through Inwood Hill Park, Riverdale, and Kingsbridge Heights.

But what do these terms mean? First, consider the fact that, while our houses stand on level ground and we generally walk on smooth, flat surfaces, the earth's understructure and the forces within it tend to distort and twist rock and create jagged mountains.

Geologists use the terms "strike" and "dip" to describe the world's contours in 3-D. "Dip" refers to the angle that rock is tilted from the horizontal, or, simply stated, how much the rock is standing at an angle that differs from lying flat. A 0° dip is a flat surface, and a 90° dip means that the rock is standing vertically, straight up and down.

It is also important to note which compass direction the rock is leaning towards. "Strike" is a measure showing the orientation of the rock on the surface.

We entered Inwood Hill Park at 207th Street in Manhattan and scurried after Dr. Feldman as he quickly walked up and down several hills for almost 3 km.

Although Manhattan schist is familiar to every local geology student, I had never been formally introduced to it. That formation has been with us since the Lower Paleozoic Era—approximately 450 MYA. Sparkling with mica, created from mud under intense heat, Manhattan Schist makes New York City skyscrapers possible by providing the solid bedrock necessary to anchor such buildings. You may notice that there are tall skyscrapers in Midtown and in Downtown Manhattan but the buildings in between are considerably shorter. In those areas with taller buildings, the Manhattan schist is close enough to the surface to provide the necessary anchorage for skyscrapers. The area in between is quite different. Formerly a valley, it was filled in with sediment deposited by water and departing glaciers, and therefore lacks the strength to support such enormous weights.

Glaciers seem far away both in time and space. However, 12,000 years ago, they covered the Inwood section of Manhattan. As we walked through the park, we saw two bits of evidence for it. In an area called "The Clove," we passed two sets of small potholes carved into the rock by the circular rotation of glacial water using rock flour (rock pulverized by grinding as the glacier moved south) as an abrasive grit. These formations were first discovered by Inwood resident Patrick Coghlan in 1931.

The second clue to that former glacial presence was a rounded boulder sitting all by its lonesome that is clearly different in its composition from any of the cliff rock nearby. These boulders are called "glacial erratics"; they are the remains of large rocks pushed forward in front of a moving glacier. Polished and rounded by the glacial movement, they are abandoned willy-nilly when glaciers recede. Since they have been dragged from afar, they do not resemble their new neighbors. The erratic we saw was composed of Palisades Diabase, an igneous (volcanic) rock, thereby, attesting to its "foreign" origin.

Across Seaman Avenue lies Isham Park, where we observed outcrops of Inwood Marble, the second of the three rock types underlying New York City. This rock was formed in the late Cambrian/Early Ordovician (c. 500 MYA). Marble is the metamorphic product of limestone after it has been subjected to great heat and pressure. The original limestone was created from huge quantities of tiny shelled creatures that sank to the ocean floor over eons.

It's easy to identify limestone. One drop of dilute hydrochloric acid on the fresh surface of a rock with a carbonate base—the shells are composed of calcium carbonate—will create fizzing.

Crossing into the Riverdale section of the Bronx, we were presented with a new formation. The Riverdale and Grand Concourse

Ridges are composed of Lower Paleozoic Fordham Gneiss, and is the oldest of the three rock types (1.1 billion years ago). We saw a sample of it at 3671 Hudson Manor Terrace where an outcrop just north of the building lies behind a fence. Made up of alternating light (feldspar)and dark bands (biotite mica), it is quite distinctive.

The "strike" of this formation is N30E (30° off north towards the east), and the "dip" is 85SE (tilted 85° towards the southeast). Further examples of this formation can be seen at Reservoir Oval and 197th Street in the Bronx. There are little pools of water on the upper surface of this outcrop where the softer stone has eroded, creating cavities in the rock.

Walking down Fieldston Road (Riverdale) is much more fun now that I can look at all the rock outcroppings with greater understanding.

Geometry Can Be Beautiful

ANYONE VISITING ISRAEL during the holiday seasons of September–October and March–April discovers that the entire country is on vacation and on the road. During the 2016 Passover holiday (March-April), radio news kept broadcasting figures for the number of visitors to the National Park system. One day, the numbers hit a record of 80,000 people. With the temperatures well above 90°F., water features were particularly popular.

That year we were vacationing in the northern part of the country, which is easy driving distance of the Golan Heights—that part of Israel to the north and east of the Sea of Galilee (Yam Kinneret). Our plans included the Hexagon Pool (*Brechat HaMeshushim*)found in the Yehudiya Nature Reserve. *Meshushim* is Hebrew for hexagon and *brecha* means 'pool.'

That trip, which ordinarily should have taken an hour and a half, took much longer. As we turned off onto the secondary road leading to the park, we realized that getting there might be the easy part. A long line of cars was already sitting along the road leading to the entrance, which had been closed. We asked the park rangers for the expected wait time. They explained that the lot was full, and that the barrier would not be raised again that day despite the fact that several cars were exiting the park. Together with other hopefuls, we nonetheless pulled over, joined the line along the side of the road, and prepared to wait. Not fifteen minutes later, the cars in front of us started entering the park, and so did we. Nary a ranger was in sight!

The gateway to the main attraction was a flat expanse filled with plantings, parked cars, and families barbecuing. Just as the summer barbecue is *de riguer* on many public holidays in the States, the barbecue—known in Israel as a *mangal*—is a requisite part of getting out into Nature for the day.

I expected that a short walk would bring us to the of basalt formation from which the park gets its name. There was, indeed, a sign pointing off to the pool, and we gamely started off.

Forty-five minutes later, after descending hundreds of feet into the ravine created by the Meshushim Stream, we reached our destination. While the ravine trail could accommodate large numbers of people along its length, the pool created by the river could only be accessed from a narrow shorefront area, so we had to wait our turn there as well. The water was cold—about 64°F.—but plenty of children and adults waded in to swim. We sat on fallen logs and enjoyed the rest, the sights, and the excitement of the children splashing in the water.

Despite interesting flora and fauna, the real attraction is the sheet-like drape of hexagonal basalt columns at the foot of the trail.

Basalt is a dark igneous rock, formed from lava, generally fine-grained, rich in iron and manganese, and low in silica. The hexagonal fracturing is the result of the cooling process after large masses of lava flow out of the Earth. Lava begins cooling immediately as it is exposed to the relatively cool air, and its mass begins to shrink. In large flows, it can fracture along the horizontal plane—that is side to side—as it begins to cool. It can, however, also accommodate shrinkage in the vertical plane—up and down—and this causes the visible columnar fracturing. Although fracturing yields primarily six-sided hexagonal columns, three, four, five, and seven-sided columns are relatively common as well. The diameter of the columns depends on the rate of cooling. Rapid cooling gives rise to small columns—those less than one centimeter, while slow cooling over many years yields columns of larger diameter.

While these columnar formations cannot be found around every corner, they are not extremely rare either. The best known formations are Devil's Postpile National Monument (California), Devil's Tower National Monument (Wyoming), the Giant's Causeway (Ireland), and Svartifoss (Iceland). The latter's formations looks eerily similar to those at the Meshushim.

Luckily for those of us living in Riverdale, the Palisades, which are particularly breathtaking in wintertime, were formed from just such jointing and can be seen from the eastern shore of the Hudson River. Hemlock Falls in Milburn, New Jersey, which involves a little hiking, is another location. Another spectacular example on the East Coast can be found in the Shenandoah National Park, Virginia.

Cretaceous Remains
Beckon from New Jersey

D OES THE PHRASE "DIGGING FOR FOSSILS" conjure up far-away places full of sandy, wind-swept cliffs? From dinosaur eggs found in the Gobi Desert, *Tyrannosaurus rex* skeletons in Colorado and elsewhere, and "supercroc" *Sarcosuchus imperator* found in both Niger and Brazil (at one time these two countries were contiguous until separated by the movement of tectonic plates), those sites live up to our romantic vision. However, I discovered that fossils can easily be found much closer to home, in less dramatic surroundings.

Several years back, we had out-of-town company which included children of differing ages. There are only so many zoo visits one can make, and I was looking around for something different. Since New Jersey has less traffic and more parking than New York City, I prefer to spend time there, all things being equal. Checking websites for "What to Do in New Jersey This Summer," I came across several fossil collection sites.

In the end, I chose to take everyone to Poricy Park in Middletown. It was about an hour's drive from Riverdale, and knowing nothing about the site but that we would be digging in a stream, we took along both sunscreen and insect repellent, boots and flip-flops, loads of towels and drinking water.

Poricy Park consists of two disconnected sections. A small parking lot just for the fossil beds is on Middletown-Lincroft Road. The park information center, however, is around the corner, on Oak Hill Road. Since it's too far to walk from one to the other, the park center should be your first stop for two reasons. For a minimal amount you can rent the equipment you will need—a trowel and a frame with a medium-size mesh screen. In addition, they will provide a sheet of simple line drawings to help identify the more likely finds.

Returning to the fossil area, you descend a very short trail into a shaded woody area, with Poricy Brook gurgling through it. The water is never higher than sixteen inches. Since you will end up getting wet anyway—even soaked—boots are unnecessary; just wear something to protect your feet in the water.

Finding fossils in the stream is very simple. You scoop up the gravelly material from the streambed with the trowel, place it on the screen and, using the brook water, wash away the mud. You are left with bits of gravel intermixed with a few fossils. These are easily recognizable from the identification sheet.

A mere glance at the sheet tells you that all the expected finds are remains from a marine environment. Your first assumption is that this is because you are panning in a stream, but these fossils are from the Cretaceous Period and are about 72 million years old. (The Cretaceous lasted from 145 to 65 million years ago and is best known as the time when dinosaurs were the dominant animals).

So why then *are* all these fossils the remains of marine animals?

The continents we know today were different in the Cretaceous and located in different latitudes. The whole area constituting today's Atlantic coastal plain was closer to the equator and more importantly, was actually a shallow ocean. Mystery solved. Fossils from Poricy include clams, squids, sponges, sharks, sea worms, even bony fishes.

There is another particularly splendid fossil-digging opportunity in New Jersey. Rowan College purchased the Inversand Quarry in Mantua. On a chosen Saturday in September every year (Sunday is the rain date), they conduct a dig which is open to the public. Finds from the site include mosasaurs, sea turtles, crocodiles, corals, and birds.

We are constantly told that the ocean floor is the most unknown place on earth. Looking backward deep into prehistory takes us into equally unknown and exciting territory!

Chasing Dead Sea Memories

M ANY YEARS AGO, WE DECIDED to take a few days' vacation at a Dead Sea hotel. Despite craving quiet and a good rest, time begins to hang heavy after a few days particularly if spa treatments are not your vice. To counter looming boredom, we signed up for a jeep tour of Harei S'dom (Mountains of Sodom), Sodom being that infamously wicked city mentioned in the Bible. The mountains run parallel to the Dead Sea for eight miles southwest of the hotel cluster, all the way to the southern end of the Dead Sea. The tour itself lasted only four hours but left an indelible impression.

The route had seemed perfectly straightforward: Drive south along the Dead Sea, turn into the first road heading west, and just keep going. I remember sinuous white chalk cliffs with stone so soft that it powders under your fingernails. I remember a fantastic white stone crater shaped by an ancient inland sea, and smooth stone corridors inviting you to explore passages of amazing beauty.

Despite trying once or twice to recreate the route and return by ourselves, we were never able to hit all the high spots and eventually, over the years, had trouble finding our way at all. Then, out of the blue, I was offered the opportunity to try retracing our route with a professional guide, and I jumped at it. A word of advice, however. Do not go to the Dead Sea in the height of the summer as we did. That day the temperature hit 110° Fahrenheit.

We met our guide, Amit, at the only gas station in the Dead Sea hotel complex, and I took meticulous notes about how and where we were driving, particularly where we entered the wild preserve. Let me say the following: You cannot do this tour except by jeep. And frankly, the sign that clearly reads *Do Not Enter* would certainly have deterred me as well. However, Amit's contention was that these signs are only meant to protect the public from wandering into a stark and unforgiving landscape without adequate preparations and knowledge.

You cannot discuss the Dead Sea area without discussing salt. In English, the words "sailor," "soldier," and "salary" are derived from the Latin *sal*. In Hebrew, the word for salt is *melach* and the Hebrew name for the Dead Sea is *Yam HaMelach*, which actually translates as "Salt[y] Sea." The Romans mined salt in the area and exported it through the ancient Philistine city of Aza (the source of the name "Gaza" today).

Salt is the overriding motif. During the Jurassic and Cretaceous Periods—which lasted 201-66 MYA—much of Israel and Syria were covered by a much larger Mediterranean Sea. The "Fish Trail" on Mt. Sodom, so called because of the fossilized fish skeletons that can be found there, provide further evidence for the ancient sea.

Over time, the water became isolated by exposed land on the west forming a lake—the Sedom Lagoon—in the low-lying valley, running north-south from the Sea of Galilee almost to the Gulf of Aqaba. This Lagoon had only a single outlet to the Mediterranean at the northern end, and salt deposits, a mile and a half thick, gradually formed at the bottom of the huge inland lake. About 2 MYA, the land on the western shore began to rise—as it continues to rise today at a rate of 0.14 inches per year—squeezing the salt together with thick sediments of shale, clay, sand, gravel, and gypsum.

The concept of salinity must come up in any discussion of the ocean or of sea water. Salinity is a measure of the amount of salt—primarily our basic table salt, sodium chloride—per liter of water. This generally corresponds to 7 teaspoons (35g) of salt per liter, giving a rate of 35 parts per thousand (ppt) or 3.5 percent salinity. The Dead Sea, whose waters feel oily due to the concentration of salt and various minerals dissolved in it, is listed at 34 percent salinity. By contrast, the Mediterranean's salinity is 3.8 percent.

Our jeep entered this dry and forbidding landscape with plenty of cold drinks and high expectations. We followed various empty streambeds—*nachal* is Hebrew for "stream"—that snake through the terrain and can foam with flash floods after a spring rainfall. The trail we followed as we entered the preserve was Nahal Hemar.

Although outside the scope of this trek, a cave on a cliff overlooking Mt. Sodom, excavated in 1983, was found filled with Neolithic materials from c. 8,310–8,110 BCE. Because of the dry local conditions, finds included wooden artifacts, basket fragments, and embroidered fabrics, in addition to the more usual bone and flint artifacts. In 2014, the Israel Museum had an exhibition of these objects; they can now be found in the permanent collection of Early Man in Israel.

Since I was looking for a specific location, I did not expect any geological novelties. But our guide was determined to give us a thorough tour, and our first stop I can only describe as 'Gills of Salt' along Nahal Sodom. This particular spot contained layers and layers of salt coating the rocks with steeple-like formations in addition to accordion-like sheets of salt, one hanging next to the other. No explanation about those formations was forthcoming, but given that there is a salt cave in the area—yes, its stalactites and stalagmites are formed from table salt through the action of miniscule amounts of rainwater percolating through the rocks—I'm guessing that the very sparse rain has something to do with the formation of these gills.

Considering the elevated temperature both outside and, unfortunately, inside the jeep, when Amit asked if we wanted to cool off, we were interested! On our own, we would never have seen the small opening into the cliff. We crawled inside and were hit with a deliciously cold 62°F. breeze. Again, because of water action, openings had been created on the cliff tops, and water percolating downward over time created chimneys in the cliffs. The temperature difference between the top of the cliffs and the cave creates a cooling downdraft. Also, there were numerous small mineral encrustations on the walls. It was truly hard to leave our cool retreat and face the heat again.

The Dead Sea receives fresh water both from the Jordan River, which flows in from the north, and from rainwater that flashes through the wadis in response to rainfall. Otherwise the wadis are just dry channels.

Before leaving the Dead Sea itself, Amit pointed out small dead trees that had been growing up out of the Dead Sea waters. He claimed that there were springs of sweet water bubbling up from underneath the saltwater that allowed for occasional plant growth. And in one spot on Nahal Hemar we saw a small lake, filled with brownish water, surrounded by a heavy growth of shrubs and small trees. This lake is apparently fed by an extensive aquifer system.

Plant life, however, can be sparse and tough in areas without waterholes and not particularly attractive in the hot months. Trying to work out the Latin names from local Hebrew ones can be difficult.

Several plants were pointed out to us. The tips of the Rose of Jericho (Anastatica hierochuntica) curl up after setting seed. Dripping a few drops of water onto those desiccated fragments leads to rapid unfurling of the branches. Curling prevents the seeds from being scattered and germinating at a time when there is no water available for growth.

There is *Anabasis articulate*, which grows in segments. Rubbing these segments with some water yields an oil that Amit claimed was good for the skin. We also saw the *Nitraria reutsa*, a small shrub whose Hebrew name, *Yamluach*, references salt and whose leaves have been used as a source of salt by desert dwellers.

But I was on this trek for one purpose only: to find the rounded crater created by that larger, ancient Mediterranean Sea. We jounced along, moving from one streambed to the next.

The final streambed, with the largest stone formations, was in Nahal Peratzim. As we moved down its stone corridors with layered towers resembling a small Grand Canyon, I recognized formations from that long-ago tour. With every turn of the *nahal*, I expected to see my crater.

Suddenly, however, we were back to where we started and again we missed it.

Afterward, I found some maps of the area and tried to piece together our route. I believe that had we continued along Nahal Peratzim into the flat plain named Mishor Amiaz (which ends at the Flour Cave), we actually would have been in the right spot.

Next time!

Landmarks from a Flood

I GREW UP ON BIBLE STORIES, and Noah and the Flood is one of the more dramatic ones. It has become fashionable to view these stories as allegories or fables, although the Flood is also a great conservation story—catastrophic habitat change, the need for enough breeding pairs, and finally repopulation when appropriate ecological conditions are restored. In any case, over the years as I started reading folk tales from around the world, it became clear that most cultures had a Flood story which certainly hints at some widespread, massive event. It has niggled in the back of my mind as an unanswered question ever since.

Several years ago we visited Yellowstone National Park, which offers a glimpse into a primordial gaseous and volcanic world. After a few days, since we were in a part of the country we had never visited before, we checked out several other National Parks and National Monuments in the area.

National Parks represent large areas protected for their scenic, inspirational, educational, and recreational value, while National Monuments contain materials of historical, cultural, and scientific interest, making them considerably more varied. National Parks can be created only by acts of Congress; National Monuments can be designated by a sitting president under the authority of the Antiquities Act of 1906, signed by Theodore Roosevelt. Many of our national parks, such as Bryce and Zion, began as national monuments.

Knowing that it was unlikely that we would ever return to Idaho, we looked around for other areas to visit. Two National Monuments were within our driving range, Craters of the Moon and Hagerman Fossil Beds. The first sounded utterly exotic, and the second coincided with my hope to see a working fossil dig.

Alas, we were disappointed to find that the fossil beds at Hagerman were no longer open to the public, due to widespread pilfering. However, we were allowed to drive to various overlooks where we could look down into the canyons, and that's when things became interesting.

One location had informational plaques reporting a massive flood, so huge as to be incomprehensible, that had caused massive erosion of solid rock in a matter of weeks. It claimed that, 15,000 years ago, water had flooded out of inland Lake Bonneville in southeastern Idaho, bursting over its rim at Red Rock Pass. That rim, which had been acting as a dam, consisted of rocky debris deposited over time by the flowing water that had created the lake. When it finally overflowed, it discharged approximately 935,000 cubic meters/sec of water, which translates into 33,000,000 cubic feet/sec, with a water depth of 2,500 feet, for eight weeks. The flood eventually ended when Lake Bonneville's height had dropped by 108 meters. Today's Great Salt Lake is considered to be a small remnant of Lake Bonneville, with a present average area of 1,730 square miles. The original Lake Bonneville was believed to have covered 32,000 square miles.

I must admit to great difficulty in conceptualizing this catastrophe. And this flood is considered to be only the *second* largest in recent times! It pales in comparison with the floods from proglacial Lake Missoula in western Montana 14,000 years ago. A proglacial lake is formed when water from a melting glacier is dammed either by glacial ice or rocky deposits left by glacial movement such as the rim at Red Rock pass.

Eastern Washington State has an area of about 1,500 square miles known as the Scablands. An unflattering term, it refers to rocky, elevated terrain that cannot be farmed. The accepted wisdom in the early 1900s was that these channeled scablands—channeled because they are full of coulees, dry riverbeds carved by water—formed slowly over eons.

Enter a colorful geologist named J Harlen Bretz, that's J without a period. He believed that the cause was the violent flow of cata-strophic amounts of water although he was not able figure out the source of such waters.

Geological orthodoxy prevailed for many years until Joseph Pardee discovered giant ripple features—some up to fifty feet in height—in the scablands' landscape that are clear evidence of the vi-olent movement of huge quantities of water. Even taking into ac-count the huge release of water, the reason the landscape could be torn up so badly was that the underlying rock was volcanic basalt, which tends to crack upon cooling. When those enormous torrents were re-leased, the sheer force produced by great quantities of speeding water simply ripped the rocks apart. In all there may have been forty dif-ferent torrents from Lake Missoula.

Several other deluges in the United States between 16,000 - 7,600 years ago may have occurred. There is also evidence that two cata-strophic floods—one 425,000 years ago and a more recent one 225,000 years—may have created the English Channel.

Who knew?

Lost Worlds in Mid-Manhattan

ON THE LAST DAY OF APRIL 2017, I had a mind-blowing expe-rience. I was again invited to join Dr. Howard R. Feldman's field trip through midtown Manhattan, this time with his Paleobiol-ogy class. We met at East 61st Street and Fifth Avenue prepared to walk to Grand Central Station (East 42nd St), examining stone fa-cades and flooring along the way. Our short walk took us through many geologic periods—from the Paleozoic (541 MYA) practically to the present.

It always amazes me what you do not see when your eye is not sensitized.

Architects use various types of stone for building facades. We saw brecciated limestone and travertine, sandstone, marble, and granite. Sandstone is probably the easiest to identify. When you touch it, it feels granular, like sandpaper, and by peering through a magnifying lens, quartz grains are visible. Anyone interested in the fine structure of natural objects should always take one along. I have a 16x loupe and it is invaluable.

Limestone and marble(metamorphosed limestone), are not difficult to identify either. You can demonstrate that a building façade is made from either by dripping a bit of dilute hydrochloric acid on it. Bubbling is the result of CO_2 gas being released through the reaction of the acid with the carbonate material of those rocks. Granite, an igneous rock, is created under pressure from cooling magma (molten lava). It can never have fossil inclusions because they could not survive the heat and pressure that created those rocks.

Our first stop was the Pierre Hotel (61st Street and Fifth Avenue), where we saw brachiopods and learned about geopetal structures. *Brachiopods* are shelled creatures constituting their own phylum, *Brachiopoda*; they can be identified by examining the shells for symmetry. Brachiopod shells are perfectly symmetrical in frontal view but asymmetrical in lateral view. *Geopetal* refers to a "way-up structure" allowing us to visualize how an organism was oriented while it was alive. In this example, the brachiopod shell is small and clearly outlined. The lower half of the fossil, where the organic part of the animal resided, became filled with sediment after death and appears dark. The upper half, once filled with gas, had become filled with a sparry cement (a bright crystalline substance), which appears white. Since the animal lived on the ocean floor, the line between the dark mud and the light-colored cement tells us which direction was up (where the sediment–water interface lay) during the animal's lifetime.

The Sherry-Netherland Hotel (59th–60th Street) has limestone frontage paneling on which you can find molds—impressions of vanished animals—of small gastropods from the family *Turritelidae*, phylum *Mollusca*, the tower shells. The elegant shell resembles a twisted cone, quite large enough for the animal to completely retreat within in times of danger.

The Plaza Hotel (59th Street and Fifth Avenue) is a symbol of elegance. However, *we* stopped to look at the outdoor limestone Pulitzer Fountain. A feathered ram ornaments the fountain and near its neck was a round figure within the stone. This turned out to be as a rudist. Again, these are molluscs that lived from the Late Jurassic to the late Cretaceous (155–65 MYA), a period of 90 million years. Using my magnifying loupe, though, I also saw tiny crinoids ossicles (more below), resembling tiny, round vertebrae.

Tiffany's attraction that day was not its jewelry but the crinoid fossils found in the limestone facade near the display windows. Crinoids, the sea lilies, belonging to phylum *Echinodermata*, have a five-fold body plan, and include more familiar creatures such as sea urchins, sand dollars, and starfish. Humans and most higher animals have bilateral symmetry. *Crinoid* comes from the Greek *krinon* meaning lily and *eidos* meaning form. The crinoid fossil resembles an upside-down umbrella with the ribs folding upward. The stems are made up of round circular structures stacked one on top of the other, called ossicles. The crinoids made their appearance in the Ordovician period—485 million years ago—and can still be found today in ocean depths below 600 feet.

Continuing south, we found a building façade that demonstrates cross-bedding; once it has been pointed out to you, you see it everywhere. These are stacks of lines in sandstone representing layers of sediment lying one above the other, laid down in different directions by wind or water. The marks can indicate ripples, dunes, and deltas and are indicative of rivers as well as tide-dominated coastal and marine settings.

St. Patrick's Cathedral is between 50th and 51st Streets on Fifth Avenue. Since the paneling around the doors is made of marble, we could not expect to find fossils, because marble is an igneous rock. This particular marble is known as the Cambrian-Ordovician Inwood Marble—also known as Tuckahoe Marble—and underlies many of the valleys in Westchester. This material was deposited approximately 500–460 MYA. The area where the deposits were found was once covered by an ocean, and the remains of marine shelled animals formed a significant deposit on the seafloor which gradually was transformed into limestone. Later, collisions of tectonic plates buried the area and subjected the limestone to tremendous pressures, converting it to marble.

Saks Fifth Avenue, at 50th Street, is also the home of two types of coral fossils—solitary and colonial—the latter forming group structures. Known as cnidarians, they are members of the *Radiata*, which, unsurprisingly, generally have a radial body plan. The name *cnidarian* come from the Greek *cnidos*, meaning stinging nettle, and refers to the cnidocysts, structures containing the stinging organelles called *nematocysts*, that allow these animals to sting and subdue their prey. This phylum also contains sea anemones, jellyfish, and sea fans. They have been part of the chain of life for the last 500 million years with some evidence indicating they go back another 200 million years. Solitary coral fossils are round, and you can easily see the internal structure. Colonial corals resemble a tight grouping of dots.

Who knew that there was an inside passage opening at 15 West 44th Street, creating an arcade exiting at 45th Street. The limestone façade of the passageway is filled with brachiopods and a few crinoids. The brachiopods here, however, have more internal definition than those we saw at the Pierre Hotel, including a structure called the *crura*. This is an internal skeletal structure that supports the *lophophore*—essentially a ring of ciliated tentacles that surround the animal's mouth and sweep food inside. Dental plates are visible on one brachiopod. These are internal plates that support the teeth in the pedicle valve, the latter being a fleshy stalk that supports some brachiopods as they grow upward like a flower from the seafloor.

Finally we turned into 42nd Street, walking east. On the south side stands a branch of the Chase Bank. Dr. Feldman challenged us to find something unusual embedded in the façade, and I spotted a bright golden sparkle that turned out to be iron pyrite, fool's gold. A sweet bit of irony!

Our tour was coming to an end as we entered Grand Central Station. The sloped flooring seemed unremarkable, but it turned out be travertine limestone. This is a common pitted stone used precisely because it is not smooth and therefore gives better traction when rain or snow outdoors make walkway conditions dangerously wet from water tracked in by pedestrians. It comes from the Later Tertiary Period—only about 20 MYA. This type of limestone is the result of calcium deposition from concentrated calcium solutions at hot springs such as those found in Yellowstone. The pitting is thought to result from the deposition of calcium around plant roots that eventually rotted away, leaving empty pits behind.

Further inside the station we saw styolites. These look like jagged, dark zigzag lines snaking through a lighter, more homogenous stone. The lines are created by pressure; material is dissolved and squeezed out of the original stone, and replaced by less-soluble materials such as clay minerals or quartz residue.

Finally there is a small brown rectangle high on the ceiling that is of completely contemporary origin. The interior of the station was cleaned a few years ago, and it was determined that the dark residue was the accumulated result of cigarette smoke. A small square was left as an object lesson on health.

Fossils can tell us so much about the environment in which they are formed. Almost everything we saw on this tour had been formed in marine environments. Partially based on the characteristics of modern members of those phyla, it is possible to glean geological insight concerning ancient conditions. We can infer the type of water, how deep it was, which direction represents the surface and undoubtedly much else.

I rarely go into Manhattan to shop, but from now on, Midtown is going to represent primarily a geological opportunity for me!

What Lies Beneath

DO YOU REMEMBER THE ORIGINAL 1959 movie *Journey to the Center of the Earth*? It follows James Mason, Pat Boone, and Arlene Dahl as they try to follow a diary's directions into the bowels of the Earth. Improbable animal life and strange adventures aside, the cave passages traveled were memorably studded with crystal formations of great beauty.

My fascination with beautiful caves may have started there but was further stoked with historical fiction describing humanity's early prehistory. I so clearly remember the enchantment of Lester Del Rey's *Cave of Spears* and much, much later, the mesmerizing *Clan of the Cave Bear* by Jean M. Auel.

As we have traveled through the United States over the years, if there was a tourist cave anywhere along our route, we always detoured to see it. While we have seen many caves with amazing speleological features, I have never seen anything that approaches the concentrated beauty of Soreq Cave located in Beit Shemesh (Israel), about twelve miles from Jerusalem. The name Soreq comes from the local waterway Nahal Soreq. The cave has an additional two names. It is called Avshalom's Cave after Avshalom Shoham, who was killed during the War of Attrition (1968–1970) between Egypt and Israel. The Hebrew name, which is the most appropriate, is M'arat HaNetifim, or "Stalactite Cave."

Despite having been to Soreq several times in the past, I am always amazed at the sheer extravagance of its beauty. You enter a huge welcoming chamber on a paved walkway. Immediately you are overwhelmed with the tremendous amount of speleothems—cave formations: stalactites, stalagmites, columns, and spaghetti strands. However, as the walkway curves to the right, seemingly rounding this huge chamber, you can see multiple smaller chambers peeking through the stone curtains. These chambers seem to fade downward, forming lower levels, and all you want to do is vault over the barrier rope and press on.

I remembered from an earlier trip, that photography was severely restricted within the cave. Like all sealed caves, this one had been effectively cut off from human contamination for eons. A whole new ecology had arisen there under conditions of perfect darkness. That ecology can be easily destroyed or severely disturbed by the entering tourists who bring with them soil contamination on their shoes, oils on their skins, and a mix of gases, including CO_2, that are exhaled with each breath. Lighting which allows the tourists to actually see all this beauty is an additional polluting factor. Therefore, the authorities try to at least limit the additional light from camera flashes. As an example of recorded changes, the relative humidity used to be 95–100 percent. Due to the large influx of visitors over the years, it has dropped to 90–95 percent.

Many caves are discovered when someone decides to check out a small opening in a wild area. Soreq's history is completely different. When you visit, you will notice local signs for the Har Tuv Quarry. In 1968, stones from that quarry were being used for the construction of the Ashdod seaport on the Mediterranean. The usual methodology was to bore holes into the stone, insert explosives, and the next day remove the broken and scattered stone and send it to the crusher.

In that year, Alex Shenberg, a mining engineer, was working at Har Tuv when a workman came to report that one of the drill holes had not successfully detonated. Upon examining the site, Shenberg saw a hole measuring two feet square. Looking through it, he saw stalactites.

He was faced with a major quandary. The property belonged to Har Tuv, but the cave seemed a priceless natural wonder. He immediately spoke with the owners and convinced them to seal it and inform the authorities.

The cave was prepared for tourists by installing walkways and lights, and opened to the public in March 1975. It is 272 feet long, 196 feet wide, and 49 feet high. It was dissolved out of dolomitic rock by acidic water action and may be 8–25 million years old, with some of the extraordinary formations thought to be 300,000 years old.

While waiting on an airport line traveling again to Israel, we started chatting with the family behind us. It was their first trip, and they were very excited. I suggested Soreq Cave as a not-to-miss attraction. I hope they went and enjoyed it as much as we did!

Marine
Animals

Wrestling with Catfish

CATFISH ARE A SOUTHERN DELICACY. However, since they are neither pretty nor kosher, they never figured among my interests, either scientific or culinary. But when something repeatedly crosses your path, it eventually makes its way into your consciousness. In this case, I have spent months investigating catfish and their effects on the environment.

In 2016 my husband and I were at the Hula Reserve in northern Israel, which is internationally famous since it's on the migration route of many bird species as they travel twice yearly between Europe and Africa.

The park itself is divided into two sections, the Reserve and the Lake (*Agmon HaHula*). While at the reserve, we observed these huge fish swimming through the channels—clearly catfish, though I had never imagined such creatures; they were easily five feet long! I thought they were pretty exciting until I found out from Reserve personnel that they are an invasive pest and cause many problems at the Hula for both migratory birds and other fish swimming in those waters. Since they grow so large, they can eat small birds and the smaller fish that would otherwise feed the migratory birds. In addition, because of their huge size none of the birds can kill and eat them. Indeed, the only predator capable of successfully hunting them is the local swamp cat (*Felis chaus*). I had been led to believe that the catfish were introduced to the Hula to keep the water clean and provide food for both migratory birds and those overwintering at the Hula. It turns out, however, that they are a native species, and very aggressive.

We returned to the States. I was intrigued by the problem but assumed that experts would eventually deal with it. Still, I frequent the local library, and shortly after our return, I chanced to pick up a documentary entitled *Okie Noodling.* "Okie" is a somewhat pejorative term referring to Oklahoma residents. I was at a loss as to the meaning of "noodling," and floored to learn that it's a sport in which men, and the occasional woman, manually pull huge catfish out of their burrows underneath the riverbank. This is quite a macho undertaking since the fish are large, very strong, and have sharp teeth. Over time, it has become a competitive sport with an annual noodling contest held in Pauls Valley, Oklahoma. The winner must present the largest live fish caught within thirty-six hours of the deadline to the judges. There are even noodling guides who will take tourists out and teach them how to handle these fish.

Mistakenly, I saw this as the answer to the Hula's problem and spoke to several guiding services about the possibility of teaching their techniques to a few Israelis, who would then help solve the problem by removing the larger fish.

I'm sure it will come as no surprised to any of my readers that the reality turned out to be much more complicated.

First of all, the fish only burrow under the banks during the breeding season, which is June–July in Oklahoma. The female digs out the burrow and lays her eggs. The male then takes over, fertilizing the eggs and guarding them until they hatch (around thirty-three hours later at around 77°F.). That, of course, means that they are less "catchable" the other ten months of the year.

I also spoke to a fish biologist from Oklahoma who explained that there are, generally, three recognized methods for catching catfish during the ten months of the non-breeding year: electro-fishing, gill netting, and trawling. He asked me which catfish species we were talking about. The Hula catfish is *Clarias gariepinus* (North African catfish). This changed the picture considerably, because these catfish do not burrow during the breeding season. They can also generate their own electric charge, which makes them too dangerous to tackle with hand-noodling techniques. He suggested that the best method to capture them would be electro-fishing, which involves stunning the fish and then scooping them out of the water. Staying out of the water, the crew remains safely insulated from electric charge by rubber gloves and boots.

Idan Barnea, the Hula Monitoring Coordinator, was kind enough to discuss their catfish problem with me. I have not yet received any updates on this problem.

Mole Crabs: Research Stars

I HAVE ALWAYS THOUGHT that I was reasonably aware of the natural world around me; yet as I am repeatedly reminded, a whole lot goes on out there, right under my nose, that I'm completely unaware of. In response to my new backyard bird feeder, which began as a whim, varieties of birds have popped up that I have never seen before. We are all familiar with robins, jays, and cardinals. But I am suddenly learning about bronze-headed cowbirds and hairy woodpeckers.

A similarly unexpected moment occurred while I was walking along the beach at Coney Island (Brooklyn, New York). It had been many years since I had been there, but, when I was much younger, I'd spent many a lazy summer day reading on a beach blanket, working on my tan. Remember those days when we thought a tan was a good idea?!

I love beachcombing! However, even then, Coney Island was a very poor choice for serious shell hunting. All I remember finding in those days were endless heaps of mussel and clam shells. So when I was out there a few weeks ago I was not expecting much of interest, but the real fun is in the hunt.

I did, in fact, find a multitude of mussel shells along with the occasional clam shell, which supported my memories. I was startled to find an oyster shell until I learned that its presence might be due to the effort to reseed nearby Jamaica Bay with oysters. But when my young grandson noticed activity in the wet sand of the swash zone, the area of breaking waves, things quickly grew infinitely more interesting.

My first reaction to anything new outdoors is to try to get a clear photo. After snapping the creature from above, we turned it over, and my first reaction was that it was a baby horseshoe crab. Horseshoe crabs (*Limulus polyphemus*) undergo several molts before becoming adults, and given the creature's legs and underside appearance, I thought it might be a juvenile form although its topside appearance did not really square with that of an adult horseshoe crab.

When in doubt, ask a professional. I called the offices of the Wildlife Conservation Society (WCS). After sending in my request together with my photo, I received a swift reply. Apparently, we had seen a mole crab, also called sand crabs, sand fiddlers, or sea cicadas. I had never heard of any of them.

Despite mole crabs and horseshoe crabs being members of the phylum *Arthropoda*, they are not closely related. Horseshoe crabs are members of family *Limulidae* and have an evolutionary history reaching back approximately 450 million years. Mole crabs are in family

Hippidae, with a shorter and murkier evolutionary history. Although no fossil mole crabs exist, the rate of molecular change in the genome implies that the family evolved before the mid to late Pliocene (5.3–2.6 MYA), so we are talking only a few million years of existence.

Mole crabs are crustaceans, members of order *Decapoda,* which includes lobsters, crayfish, shrimp, and krill. In Greek, *deca* means ten and *pod* means foot, and, indeed, they have five pairs of legs. They form an important part of the diet of both sea and shore birds, as well as fish. Despite heavy predation, mole crab maintain their numbers because females can lay up to 45,000 eggs each from February to October. The eggs drift out to sea and hatch about a month later. Four to five months later, they reach maturity.

Mole crabs are found both in ocean waters and on shore in the swash zone, coming ashore as wave riders. Using only their hind feet they bury themselves quickly in the sand, leaving just their eyes and antennae exposed. As the waves recede, they uncoil their antennae and attempt to feed on the plankton present in the water flowing past.

Since mole crabs are filter-feeders, they are sentinels for domoic acid, the neurotoxin produced by algae that is concentrated by shellfish and causes amnesic shellfish poisoning in humans. The term "amnesic" refers, among other things, to memory problems that can be caused by this poison. Scientists therefore use mole crab tissue to measure amounts of domoic acid in the local sea water. The mole crab is also used as a research tool in neurological studies because they have the largest sensory neurons in the animal kingdom.

Many aquariums now have "touch tanks" where children and adults can safely handle small sea creatures such as sea urchins, rays and starfish. Mole crabs might make a fine addition!

Surprising Elephant Seals

NEVER BE TOO SMUG about what you think you know about Nature! A few weeks ago, while overseas, we were looking through a friend's photo book who had visited the West Coast. I was browsing the captions in Hebrew and understood one of them to say that elephant seals (genus *Mirounga*) molt once a year. Because my Hebrew isn't perfect and English is not their native tongue, I was amused, because mammals do not molt—and I said so. Big mistake! To be fair to my friends, I decided to check this out and discovered, not only that elephant seals do molt once a year, but that it is such a complete and major process, in which they lose all their old fur and epidermal skin, that it is called a "catastrophic molt." I was most embarrassed, but it was also an opportunity to learn something new and interesting.

The molting process in elephant seals lasts twenty-five to twenty-eight days during which time the animals do not feed, since they do not go into the water. There are different molting schedules depending on age and gender. Females and juveniles molt from April to May, sub-adult males from May to June, and adult males from July to August.

By definition, molting is accompanied by fasting. There is a second 25–28 day period when these seals fast: during the birthing–mating period. At that time, they are in the general California area. At all other times of the year, the seals feed far offshore.

Elephant seals get their name from the pendulous nose, or proboscis, of the males. This feature develops upon sexual maturity, between three and five years of age, and is used in the mating "dance." In order to establish dominance, males will inflate the nose and produce a drum-like noise warning away subordinate males.

Northern elephant seals are a conservation success story. They were being slaughtered wholesale for their blubber, which the animals need for storing energy, insulation against the cold, and buoyancy, and which was being rendered into oil for the production of soap, margarine, cosmetics, and oil-burning lamps. By 1892, the population had plummeted from hundreds of thousands to fewer than 120 animals. In 1922, the Mexican government—since the seals were then found on Guadalupe Island, off Baja—designated them a protected species. As they increased in numbers and moved north into American California, the U.S. government followed suit. Today, the population is estimated at 160,000 animals.

If there are Northern Elephant Seals, then it is not surprising that there are Southern Elephant Seals. The southern animals are found in Antarctic and sub-Antarctic waters, feeding on the rich marine life that thrives in those waters. The northern seals, meanwhile, will move further north after mating to feed in the waters off northern Washington State and Vancouver Island, British Columbia.

Hard as it may be to imagine, elephant seals spend the bulk of their lives in the water. The Northern females come ashore to give birth to their young in December, delivering one pup, which weighs about 75 pounds at birth and will grow to 250–350 pounds in the 25–28 days that the mother will nurse it. She will then wean the pup simply by returning to the water, leaving the pup to learn on its own how to swim and hunt.

The females are receptive to the males about 24 days after giving birth. The fertilized egg, though, remains in a state known as delayed implantation in which the embryo does not implant in the uterus but instead remains dormant for several months. Other animals that employ this gestational method include bears, kangaroos, weasels, and badgers.

Classically, molting refers to the process whereby skin, the pelage (hair, feather, fur, or wool), or some other body part is shed. Dog owners find more hair shed as the cold months yield to spring warmth, and birds change their plumage. Sometimes an empty snake skin will appear in the garden. Lizards, frogs, and salamanders apparently molt as well.

I am more familiar with insect molting which is required as the insect grows larger and needs to shed its exoskeleton (outer skeleton) to accommodate further growth. Most impressively, of course, butterflies change from wormlike caterpillars to the beautiful creatures whose body parts have no identifiable relation to those of the caterpillar.

So this week a misconception turned into a major and enjoyable learning experience for me.

Sea Silk and the Golden Fleece

WE WERE AT THE ENDPOINT of our recent road trip having arrived at Sanibel Island located off the west coast of Florida. If you've never heard of it, Sanibel Island is renown as a destination for serious shellers—beachcombers with a purpose.

Wherever we travel, if a seashore is nearby, I spend a few hours checking it out and I'm always asking traveling friends to keep me in mind whenever they visit a beach filled with shells. Far too many areas, though, are completely barren. Coney Island is almost bare, friends came up empty in Hawaii, and the beaches in Tel Aviv yield only a limited number of species and precious few specimens.

Immediately upon arrival, I hurried down to the shore. The best time for shelling is an hour before low tide—of which there are two every day—to an hour after low tide. Therefore, tide charts are available everywhere on the island.

What makes Sanibel such a good location for finding seashells? It's on the Gulf side of Florida and, in that location, the Gulf tide flows north from the Caribbean. Sanibel is arc-shaped lying east to west across this flow. In addition, there is no sharp drop-off in the offshore water level where a high underwater shelf would effectively create a wall preventing the shells from reaching the beach entirely. With a gradual slope rising landward, shells wash up onto shore allowing avid shellers the opportunity to make a great find!

Along the main drag is the Bailey-Matthews National Shell Museum, a must for the dedicated beachcomber. The museum provides a laminated sheet showing all of the 149 different shell types that have been collected on Sanibel. In the end, I found only fifteen varieties in the enormous heaps of shells scattered everywhere along the shore. But when I suggested to one of the naturalists at the Museum that I was particularly disappointed not to have found a Junonia (*Scaphelia junonia*), a cream shell with twelve spiral rows of squarish brown dots, I learned that everybody else is looking for this rare find as well. Apparently, this gastropod mollusk—named for the Roman goddess Juno—lives in deep tropical waters many miles away and is only washed ashore by very severe storms, which were certainly not on my vacation agenda.

The museum exhibits shells from around the world as well as many examples of how shells have been used—as jewelry, as currency, and even buttons. One of the cases I examined discussed sea-silk, a term that I had only recently run across and seemed very intriguing.

One of the shells on display was of a mussel colloquially called a "pen shell" (genus *Atrina*, family *Pinnidae*), a bivalve mollusk. A related genus is *Pinna*, an endangered Mediterranean species that includes the extremely large and long-lived *Pinna nobilis*, which can grow up to four feet in length and live up to twenty years in beds of sea grass. Both mollusk species develop as tiny, free-swimming larvae after fertilization. Later, they form a calcareous shell and drop to the bottom of the seafloor, attaching themselves by a tuft of byssus threads secreted by a special gland in the foot. The byssus of the *Pinna nobilis* has been used since antiquity to create an extremely fine, golden thread for small luxury items of clothing. Based on some ancient sources, Jason's Golden Fleece, of mythological fame, may actually have been a mass of these byssus fibers.

Joyce Matthys, a Sanibel native, decided to replicate the project using the local *Atrina* mollusks. This project became enormously time-consuming. First, she had to collect enough byssus from the three local species, *Atrina rigida*, *Atrina serrata* and *Atrina seminuda*. Byssus threads remain attached only to the living animal, so an empty shell washed up on the beach was useless. In addition, the fibers are quite short, such that a single tuft does not yield much material, and even that is fouled with dirt and debris. The second step, therefore, was to wash the harvest with Dawn dishwashing liquid or with shampoo. Next, the threads had to be combed. In the end, it took her five years to accumulate enough material to spin the byssus into yarn. The final stage was crocheting the yarn into a small fabric rectangle, which needed a final rinse in an acidic liquid—Joyce chose pure lemon juice—so that it would gleam in sunlight.

There has been renewed scholarly interest in this material including conferences and traveling exhibits.

There Are Whales in New York! Really?

I HAVE ALWAYS ASSOCIATED WHALE-WATCHING with vacationing far from New York. However, since I have been known to get seasick on ferries, I have had little incentive to check out anything remotely involving heaving water. But in a fit of whimsy I bought two tickets to an American Princess Whale Watching Cruise out of Riis Landing in Breezy Point, New York, for four hours, hopefully, of whale-watching.

The day we chose was one of the most gorgeous summer days imaginable. The air was spectacularly clear, the water a shade of blue that you would like to wear draped around your shoulders and, just with me in mind, wonderfully calm.

I was pleasantly surprised to find out that it was more than an opportunity to see whales. With two naturalists aboard, it was not only fun but extremely educational. It turns out that American Princess Tours is the commercial arm of a scientific endeavor called Gotham Whale, founded in 2006 by Paul Sieswerda and intended to track and identify whales, seals, and dolphins living and migrating in New York Bay and the Western New York Bight between Long Island and the coast of New Jersey. A "bight" is a bend in a coastline or river and is distinguished from a bay by being shallower.

Humpback whales were common in pre-Colonial times but vanished from these waters long ago. There are several reasons generally cited for their presence now. The first is the significant improvement in water quality. The second could well be the result of the humpback's luck to have been one of the first species listed in the Endangered Species Conservation Act. Lastly, there's the availability of high-quality food, since they need to consume about 3,000 pounds of food daily. One particular fish species that entices whales is men-haden, a very oily fish used extensively in the production of fish oil capsules found on the supplement shelf.

To help improve the chances of successful sightings, small scout ships ranged ahead of us, seeking either the whales themselves or schools of menhaden. These fish masses could be spotted—once we knew what we were looking at—by water turbulence at the surface shaped roughly like a twenty-foot-long oval, with the water sparkling just so off the myriad tiny fins flicking above the surface. The scout ships report likely locations, and the tour boat moves along to those spots to check things out. In the end, we spotted whales four different times.

The important question for the naturalists was, "Are all these sightings one whale or some number from one to four different whales?" This is where the citizen-scientist aspect of Gotham Whale kicks in. The simplest way to describe this movement is: "There's a big world out there and relatively few scientists available or interested in any given project." With the vast numbers of interested citizens available who are already making observations, scientists can collect more data more quickly the more eyes there are on the ground. Tour participants are invited, and expected, to share their photographs with Gotham Whale, and these photos can be used to make individual identifications.

Just as fingerprints are unique among human, zebra-stripe patterns are unique to each zebra, the same is true of fluke pigmentation and scarring. Comparisons of photos allow scientists to declare with great certainty how many humpbacks have actually moved north for the summer.

From an initial number of five sightings in 2011—who might have been the same individual—the number has swelled to a hundred individuals in 2014. Indeed, there is one whale they call "Rockaway Jerry" who is readily recognized by the naturalists and is regularly seen. He received this name because he was first spotted on Jerry Garcia of the Grateful Dead's birthday. The humpbacks migrate to New York in the summers to fatten up on the rich food resources here and return to the West Indies in the winter for breeding and calving.

The times they are a'changin on the West Coast as well. Out there, instead of humpbacks, we find gray whales. They traditionally calve near Baja in the summer and migrate to the rich feeding grounds in the Arctic during the winter. Although there is evidence that gray whales once lived in the Atlantic, they vanished from there long ago. Now, however, the Pacific population can migrate to areas where they have long been absent, because the ice is melting in Arctic waterways, allowing them passage back to the Atlantic. Recently, there was a sighting of a single gray whale along the coast of Israel who then moved on to Spain. Another gray whale was also sighted off the coast of Namibia.

Since this cruise went so well, I may venture out soon to see the seals as well!

Plants

As Thrilling as Botany Gets

I N 2018 THERE WAS A BREATHLESS WATCH going on in the Conservatory of the York Botanical Garden (NYBG) in anticipation of the blooming of the *Amorphophallus titanum* flower, formerly the official flower of the Bronx. There was even a video cam relaying the situation to an excited public in real time.

One of several outstanding characteristics of this flower, known tastefully as the corpse flower, is the extraordinary stench it exudes when it blooms. The nickname is not much of a stretch, because the smell is reminiscent of rotting meat. Having encountered the vile odors of ginkgo fruit, skunk, and the occasional dead bird, I had no intention of racing to smell something so clearly advertised as deadly. Instead, I went to see the flower structure as it appeared *before* opening, and that was quite remarkable in itself.

The flowering specimen and two juveniles of different ages were sitting on a platform in the pool right immediately inside the Conservatory entrance. All eyes were on the greenish bud, which was several feet tall and wrapped in layers of a petal material pleated at the upper edge. The *Amorphophallus* is a member of the *Araceae* family, in which the reproductive organ is a spike (called a *spadix*), wrapped in a covering (called the *spathe*) creating a waterproof bag. The flowers and pollen structures are contained in two separate rings around the base of the spadix. If the flowers are fertilized, multiple red fruits will form, and later the seed. Since the plant is not self-fertile, another male specimen has to provide the female structures with necessary pollen. The plant ensures that it cannot self-fertilize by having the female flowers open a day before its own pollen is released. While we may be bemused by so terrible a stench emitted by something as remarkable as a flower, the natural pollinators of the *Amorphophallus* are beetles and flies, which presumably find such odors attractive.

The huge public interest was probably due to the rarity of the event and the sheer size of the flower—the entire structure can reach 12 feet—and its uniqueness. The stench merely comes along for the ride although one eager visitor said that she was "interested in the full experience."

While this is not the first *Amorphophallus*-flowering event at NYBG, it has not happened in many years. A plant acquired in 1932 bloomed only in 1936, and a second one acquired in 1935 bloomed in 1939. The present specimen was acquired in 2007 and has been growing in the Nolen Greenhouse in a room designed for tropical plants. While in its growth stage, it is watered and fertilized heavily. During initial growing years, the plant could easily be mistaken for a small tree with a slender green trunk, topped by three separate leaf fronds. Surprisingly, that entire tree-like structure is actually a single leaf, those fronds simply being leaflets that supply the corm (an underground storage organ) with food. The size of that leaf increases with the age of the plant. At the end of each growing cycle, the leaf crumples and dies away, and the plant goes into a dormancy period during which it is not watered at all, although it will be repotted. After several months of dormancy, new growth pushes up from the roots; only then does watering and fertilizing recommence. Only upon seeing this new growth does it become clear whether the plant is putting out a new leaf as in the previous year or going into its magical flower form. After a successful bloom, the plant will revert to growing as its leafy form for many years until an unknown internal signal sets off the next blooming cycle.

Altogether, to get a flower, is generally a ten-year-plus project and not for anyone who needs instant gratification.

Babies are born when they are good and ready. It seems the *Amorphophallus* feels no greater urgency to blossom. The one everybody was watching was a week overdue when I wrote this entry, although the blooming process seemed to have started. Maybe next time I'll go see it in its full stinking glory.

The *Amorphophallus* flower finally bloomed and after thirty-six hours, the huge spathe closed up again, leaving NYBG to settle down for the next ten years. . .until *Amorphophallus* blooms again.

I had the privilege of volunteering at NYBG for several years and usually worked in the succulent/cactus room at the Nolen Greenhouse. Tuesday, after the blooming, I came as usual and found the huge *Amorphophallus* inflorescence sitting quietly in its pot in a hallway. The spadix looked somewhat the worse for the wear, but the whole plant was intriguing to see up close. I expected that it be returned to its normal growing area and essentially retired.

Later, a whole group of people were standing around it with an air of eager anticipation. There were people from Public Relations who were preparing live-streaming videos for the NYBG Facebook page. The videos were intended to document all the steps that the scientists at the Garden were going to take to preserve material from the spent inflorescence for future research.

I already told you that the *Amorphophallus* is not self-fertile. In an effort to obtain seed from the NYBG bloom, attempts had been made to obtain pollen from another botanical garden with its own blooming plant. Regrettably, the pollen did not arrive on time, and the NYBG plant could not be fertilized. However, that does not mean that its *own* pollen could not be harvested to be sent onward to another garden, where it could be put to good use. Marc Hachadourian, Manager of the Nolen Greenhouses for Living Collections, cut open the inflorescence to remove pollen, which was shipped immediately to two other botanical gardens with *Amorphophalli* on the verge of blooming. Later, these gardens will in turn harvest pollen and send it to yet other gardens, paying the gift forward as it were, so that, with any luck, some of these flowers can be successfully fertilized to produce viable seed from which new plants will be grown.

Using a razor, Hachadourian first cut a window into the spathe, which was about three-quarters of an inch thick and resembled watermelon rind. Since the last *Amorphophallus* bloom was in 1939, this was a first-time experience for himself and all those present. Everybody crowded around, peering intently into a seemingly secret chamber. Cutting completely around the base of the spathe, he removed it entirely, revealing the inner structures. He described the upper part of the spathe as having a rubbery texture. The pollen structures lie in a ring above the female flowers. First, he brushed the pollen downward by hand onto a sheet of paper. Since that did not yield much material, he switched to a paintbrush to reach inside and wipe off more pollen, which had already shaken loose from the anthers and was clinging to the unreceptive female structures.

The top of the spadix, when opened, resembled a loofah sponge filled with a network of fibers. A cross-section of the base of the spadix resembled a squash pith, although the plants are not related, and the texture of the sections through the female structures felt like Styrofoam.

Then Daniel Atha, Conservation Program Manager, took over. The next step was to preserve the plant materials in a way that would show future botanists how the plant actually looked, so that scientists could learn how to identify future specimens. That process involved cutting off pieces from various parts of the plant—the spathe with the frilly, red upper lip and the top eight inches of the spadix—and preparing a herbarium sheet.

To do so, the plant material is first laid out on a sheet of newspaper which is then folded over the specimen. Newsprint is used because it is excellent for wicking out moisture. This packet is then laid upon a sheet of paper 11.5 x 16.5". This sandwich is then placed in a press and subjected to an artificial heat source to drive out all the moisture. The paper sheet is later stored in the Herbarium, a collection of plant specimens much like a library, where it will be available for further study.

The second process, used to preserve material for DNA studies, involved storing some of the material in silica gel. The third process, which is intended to preserve material for use in morphological-anatomical studies, consisted of immersing slices of male and female tissue in a preservative solution composed of formaldehyde, acetic acid, and ethanol, which will maintain the material indefinitely.

How lucky for me that I happened to be in the right place at the right time to see the blooming sequel!

Bleeding Hearts

IF YOU WENT TO SCHOOL in the Fifties and Sixties, do you remember how poetry was an integral part of the curriculum? We had to learn poems by heart and later write them out stanza by stanza, complete with punctuation. I want to consider the spring-blooming plant we call bleeding hearts, which reminds me of the Joyce Kilmer poem "Trees." It opens:

> *I think that I shall never see*
> *a poem as lovely as a tree.*

I hear an echo of this phrase when I look at bleeding hearts flowers:

> *I think that I shall never see a flower*
> *as wondrous as thee.*

The plant is also known as the lyre flower, an obvious nickname upon close examination of the flower. Another nickname, lady-in-the-bath, is not particularly obvious until you turn the flower photo upside down. This very extraordinary flower is composed of a total of four petals, the outer ones pink and the inner ones white.

When I began gardening, I bought a few plants through mail order which I expected to look like the standard bleeding heart with racemes full of intricate flowers. Racemes are long stems with flowers arranged separately and equidistant along the stem. However, those plants did not turn out to be the large flowering versions that I expected. I had, in fact, bought a relative, *Dicentra eximia*, which is a perfectly nice low plant with fern-like leaves, which still resides in my garden. But it has not proven to be very dynamic in its ability to spread, nor has it reseeded itself elsewhere in the garden.

Frankly, if I'm going to buy a plant, I want it to make itself worthwhile by reproducing at a reasonable rate so an initial small investment yields some noticeable return. Hostas are a good example of a plant that is great in the shade, has many colorful cultivars, and can be propagated every few years. Propagation of hostas involves subdivision of the plants which is a more of an effort than having your plant reseed themselves with wild abandon, but the results are so good that I now have so many hostas that I am giving away plants to eager friends.

Incidentally, one of the great benefits of making new friends based on love of plants is that people are delighted to share their surplus and are happy to find someone interested in giving a favorite plant a good home. Sometimes, identification of such gifts is unclear, and it may take a while to properly identify a flower.

In any case, the following year, when I happened to be in a garden center, I saw some very large bleeding heart plants—*Dicentra spectabilis* (changed to *Lamprocapnos spectabilis* in 2011). I bought three and carefully planted and watered them. They were indeed lovely as long as they flowered, but afterward they just disappeared. I decided that enough was enough and that whatever they needed I could not adequately provide and I would just move on.

Imagine my surprise the next spring when three even larger plants popped up—and they all seemed to be doing very well. It seems that bleeding hearts are spring ephemerals, plants that bloom early in the season, die back once the temperatures rise in the summer, and re-bloom the following spring. In the case of bleeding hearts, however, the foliage may continue growing all season if planted in the shade and adequately watered.

As the seasons passed, I learned more about these plants. One fall, I was digging a hole to plant some new acquisition and was startled to see that I was digging up some unidentified roots. I quickly realized that I must have chosen just the spot where the springtime bleeding hearts had been growing. Since the damage was already done, I took the root pieces and planted them around my garden, hoping that they would just go ahead and do something beneficial for me. It turned out to be a useful experiment, since I found healthy bleeding hearts all over the property the following spring. I later came to realize that the mature plants were also setting seed when I began to find baby plants all over the garden.

My plants are now past peak, but I can still see those wonderful flowers peeking out at me through the surrounding foliage, and I look forward to greeting them upon their return next spring.

That Sharp Taste Is Capers

WHEN I WAS YOUNGER, I was familiar mostly with the pumpkin pie spices—cinnamon, cloves, nutmeg, and the like. However, mixing in different circles as time went on, I one day found myself at a barbecue hosted by a serious foodie. The selection of meats and salads was both generous and beautifully presented. I filled my plate and joined friends at a table, prepared for an enjoyable meal. I tasted the various unfamiliar dishes. Imagine my surprise when I took a bite of what was clearly potato salad incorporating a completely unrecognizable taste. I took another small bite and realized that the small, round, green "somethings" in the salad were the source of my surprise. That was my introduction to the caper.

The comedian Jackie Mason has a funny monologue about "acquired tastes" among the *avant-garde*. He points out that no one seems to need to acquire a taste for chocolate. While I will admit that, over time I have indeed acquired a taste for formerly unpalatable foods, capers had never made it onto my list.

Apparently, there are two caper spice possibilities—one is the flower bud, the other the berry, both of which are generally pickled for use. The one I so unhappily encountered was a bud.

The caper, a Mediterranean plant, can be found growing wild all over Israel and has a most beautiful flower. Recently, I found a small plant growing from between the stones of a Jerusalem wall. It is highly tenacious and can survive both arid conditions and rough handling. Even cutting it back to the roots will not effectively kill it, so the caper has become a metaphor for endurance.

Its botanical name is *Capparis spinosa*. Its place of origin is not clear though one hypothesis is that *Capparis* may refer to the island of Cyprus—*Kypros* in Greek—where they grow abundantly. *Spinosa*, "thorny," derives from a pair of hooked spines at the base of each leaf stalk.

The caper has been known since ancient times and was used then as a carminative. Apparently, that means that it was used as a digestive aid for the elimination of flatulence and, in fact, has nothing to do with the word "carmine," which is a vivid shade of red. The Latin root is *carminate*—"healing through use of a charm"—which eventually found its way into English as the word "charm."

Because of the caper's importance in various Mediterranean cuisines, it is now being cultivated in addition to being foraged in the wild. There are farms in Morocco, Turkey, and the southeastern Iberian Peninsula, as well as many other locations around the Mediterranean basin. In the United States, San Marco Growers in California supplies local California nurseries with plants. The plants, should you be able to buy them somewhere in New York, are root-hardy only to about 18°F. That means that there is a strong likelihood, given some of our extreme winter weather conditions, they will not be perennial in our area.

Unopened buds should be harvested only on dry days. The plants can be repeatedly hand-picked every 8 to 12 days, which generally allows for 9 to 12 collections per growing season. The buds are then wilted and packed in white vinegar. Alternatively, they can be processed over the course of a week with fine sea salt and will then keep for a year.

Capers belong to the botanical group called *Rosids*—which, not surprisingly, includes roses, although theirs is only a distant relationship. There are examples of fossil *rosids* from the Cretaceous Period (125–99.6 MYA). *Rosids* are part of the Order *Brassicales*, which includes the pungent mustard and cabbage families. The outstanding characteristic of this group is the production of mustard-oil compounds. It is these compounds, released from both the caper bud and berry during processing, that are responsible for the caper's unique and strong flavor.

Every time we are in Israel, we make a trip to the Western Wall in Jerusalem, which is the only remnant of the Holy Temple. It comprises forty-five courses of huge limestone blocks with seventeen courses below ground and twenty-eight above, rising sixty-two feet into the air. Growing between many of the blocks are small scrubby plants that I was never able to identify; I was surprised to discover that they are, in fact, caper bushes.

The Varieties of Crocus Experience

C ROCUSES ARE THE ICONIC SPRING FLOWER. Although we see the tips of daffodils long before the end of winter, the first flowers to spring up are the colorful, cheerful crocus that opens in the bright sunlight and closes up again as the sun moves towards the horizon, only to reopen the next day. That spring crocus, *Crocus vernus*, grows white, purple, and yellow flowers and is a particular delight when planted in masses on sloping hills. The fact that crocus is synonymous with glee, youthfulness, and cheerfulness probably comes as no surprise particularly upon learning that *vernus* is the Latin word for "youthful" and was once a boy's name. The name "crocus" comes from the Latin adjective *crocatus* for the particular shade of yellow called "saffron."

However, our spring crocus, planted in the fall and so delightful, is not the source of the very expensive spice we call "saffron" that is used extensively in various cuisines, including Spanish, French, and Persian. The saffron plant, is a crocus relative named *Crocus sativus*—*sativus* being Latin for "cultivated." It too is planted in the fall, but it will not bloom until the following fall. The *sativus* suffix used as the species epithet may refer to the fact that the plant is sterile in the same way that the mule, offspring of a horse and a donkey, is sterile, so *Crocus sativus* depends on vegetative propagation by human hands. This is accomplished by digging up the corms—a part of the stem that grows underground and that is reinforced with fibrous threads, not to be confused with bulbs, which are layered structures—and removing and planting the baby corms for a new crop of vigorous plants the next year.

Saffron is one of the world's oldest and most expensive spices. The spice itself comes from the three blood-red stigmas in the center of the flower, which are the female structures. Since these plants are sterile, they do not produce pollen, and the stigmas cannot be pollinated. Instead, over the two-week period during which crocus fields bloom, gatherers go into the fields and pluck out these stigmas with tweezers. They are then dried and sealed in light-tight packets to maintain the spice's longevity. It requires more than 70,000 flowers which in turn need one square kilometer of land to yield one pound of saffron-producing stigmas, which explains their hefty price tag. Saffron is also graded. Less-expensive grades are available, but they may be adulterated with other plant parts which lack spiciness.

Throughout history saffron has been used, not only as a spice, but as a medication, as a dye, a perfume ingredient, and a pigment. When the color saffron is mentioned, many of us think first of the saffron-colored robes of Buddhist monks. These days those robes are actually dyed with a resin from trees of the Gamboge (*Garcinia*) family, because saffron is far too costly to use for dyeing, if indeed it was ever used for that purpose.

Saffron has been known to humanity for a surprising long time. Fifty thousand years ago, it was being employed as an ingredient of a red pigment found in cave-paintings in Iraq. There is also reference to it in a botanical treatise compiled for the Assyrian king Ashurbanipal (7th century BCE). Minoan frescoes, painted 3,600 years ago, show the gathering of saffron.

We have taken our children blueberry picking, but saffron-gathering seems to be very hard work!

Daffodils and Their Lovely Relatives

WITH THE WEATHER WARMING at the end of February 2017 and the sudden appearance of some early-flowering bulbs, I fully expected to see drifts of daffodils. The tips of their leaves had been visible for months, growing incrementally but steadily. A recent heavy snowfall, however, temporarily halted further blooming of many spring plants. But the daffodils had not been vanquished; they struggled on in the face of sudden inclement weather. After checking around the neighborhood as well as the New York Botanical Garden, I could safely report that they were undaunted and would be captivating us shortly with their glow of yellow sunshine.

Have you ever noticed how many of the early flowering plants are yellow? These include winter aconite (*Eranthis hyemalis*), the native marsh marigold (*Caltha palustris*) and its evil invasive twin the lesser celandine (*Ranunculus ficaria*), daffodils (*Narcissus*), and forsythia (Genus *Forsythia*). Current speculation revolves, as usual, around the pollinators, in this case flies, bees, butterflies, and hawkmoths. Insects and mammals make use of different parts of the light spectrum, with many of the pollinating insects operating in the range of ultra-violet light. The flowers, therefore, exploit this predilection by creating patterns visible only in ultra-violet, which we humans, unfortunately, cannot see. In the case of yellow flowers, ultra-violet makes the yellow appear blue and frequently creates the semblance of a bullseye in the flower's center, where the reproductive structures are located. Anything that makes a flower more attractive to a pollinator obviously increases the rate of pollination. Reproduction is the ultimate role of the flower, in order to ensure the next generation of plants through fertilization and finally seed production.

Today's burning question, however, is, "What is the actual difference between daffodil, narcissus, and jonquil?" since all three terms tend to pop up almost interchangeably. Research indicates that this is primarily a semantic issue. Although all of these flowers belong to the genus *Narcissus*, the general term "daffodil" refers to all the various flower types, while "jonquil" refers only to a specific subtype—those having a fragrant, multi-flowered stem with a short, flared center.

Given the popularity of daffodils and the multitude of cultivars available in the market, it is not surprising that there is a national gardening society devoted solely to daffodils—the American Daffodil Society. Established in 1954, its purpose is to promote research into the genus *Narcissus*, to create more daffodil enthusiasts, register new cultivars, and work internationally on issues of classification and act as a clearinghouse for all matters pertaining to daffodils.

They have also established three awards for American hybridizers. The William C. Pannil Award goes to a named standard that has shown outstanding qualities for a minimum of five years after registration. The John and Gertrude Wister Award recognizes an outstanding daffodil that demonstrates continuing vigor and beauty in the garden. And the Innovation Gold Medal is awarded to the most innovative new daffodil exhibited at the American Daffodil Society's (ADS) National Show.

Every time I open a catalogue for spring-flowering bulbs, I am overwhelmed by the variety offered with numerous variations in color as well as in the shape of the perianth and the corona. The *perianth* consists of the petals, and the *corona* is the tube-like structure in the flower's center surrounding the stamen and pistils. The ADS uses a classification system developed by the Royal Horticultural Society of the United Kingdom (RHS) . It should be noted, however, that the color-coding system is derived from work by Tom Throckmorton of Des Moines, Iowa, who was both a physician and an award-winning horticulturalist known as the "Dean of Daffodils."

The RHS classification of daffodils uses several characteristics: the color of various parts of the perianth as well as the corona, number of blooms on a stem, size of the corona relative to the perianth, number of units making up the perianth and the corona, and the angles of perianth in relation to the corona. This has yielded twelve categories of hybridized flowers and a thirteenth reserved for non-domesticated plants.

One of the best reasons to plant daffodils is that squirrels and deer will not eat them. The bulbs and foliage contain a poison called lycorine as well as calcium oxalate crystals, a serious irritant present in many plant species. These compounds make them occasionally dangerous to humans as well who have cooked them mistaking them for onions.

The *Narcissus* are members of the *Amaryllidaceae* family and have been with us since the late Oligocene/early Miocene—approximately the last 23 million years. They are native to the Iberian Peninsula. The genus name derives from the Greek legend of the beautiful youth named Narcissus who fell in love with his reflection and drowned in a pool of water, reaching for his image.

> *And then my heart with pleasure fills,*
> *And dances with the daffodils.*
> —William Wordsworth

Daylilies Pop, Pop, Pop in Local Gardens

ANYWHERE YOU WALK at around the end of spring, be it cultivated gardens or scrub waste, you cannot miss the profusion of orange blossoms of the wild daylily we called tiger lilies as children. Little did I know then that each bud bloomed for only a single day, and that the extended bloom period was the result of numerous blooms opening sequentially on a single branched stalk.

Another common variety is the yellow Stella D'Oro daylily. Together these two plants are workhorses, growing well under challenging conditions. Many home gardeners cherish them for their ability to quickly colonize a difficult spot. The flip side, of course, is that, when you finally want to tackle that spot, it's hard to rid yourself of them. My solution, in absolute desperation, was to cut off the foliage as it repeatedly appeared until the roots finally gave out although it still took several years to finally banish daylilies from that spot. Because of these hardy qualities, the plant has now been officially designated an invasive species.

As you already know, a hint that a flower is popular is the existence of a flower society dedicated solely to it. The scientific name for daylilies is *Hemerocallis*, and the daylily society is the American Hemerocallis Society (AHS), which offers an astonishing amount of information on all the varied characteristics of this plant. Scrolling down the screen, particularly the "Frequently Asked Questions," was an eye opener.

The original work of hybridizing was done by Dr. Arlow Burdette Stout, Curator of Education and Laboratories at the New York Botanical Gardens (NYBG). He began working there in 1911 and, over the ensuing thirty-seven years, crossed 50,000 daylilies and registered ninety-seven hybrids. He developed the first red daylily, which was quite a feat considering that the only colors originally available were orange and yellow. Today the color spectrum runs pretty much from lavender to near white. The flowers have also developed many petal types—colored edges and ruffles—as well as midribs. Part of the daylily walk at NYBG is named the Arlow B. Stout Garden.

On the AHS website, I was delighted to learn of two additional qualities that are personally grabbing. The first is called *polychrome*, in which the flower segments have an intermingling of three or more colors, such as yellow, melon pink, and lavender. The second is called *dusting*, which refers to a glitter-like quality on the petal surface. If the sparkles are white, then it is considered *diamond* dusting; if golden, they are *gold* dusted.

Hybridizing may sound painstaking and therefore too difficult for home gardeners. Not at all! All you need are two parent plants. Although each plant has both pollen and ova, daylilies, fortunately, do not self-fertilize. Look carefully at a newly opened bud, and you will see the yellow pollen grains all over the anthers. Remove the anther by pulling it gently by hand and then just dab the pollen all over the pistils of other plants. A seed pod will develop over the next few weeks, and the seed will be ripe for planting 45–50 days after fertilization, when the seed pod cracks open and you can see the shiny black seeds inside. Michael Ruggiero, formerly Senior Horticulturist at NYBG, recommends just putting them in an envelope and keeping them in the refrigerator until spring.

Since 1950, AHS has awarded the Stout Silver Medal in honor of Dr. Stout. In a lengthy process, the new cultivar must win first an Honorable Mention Award and then an Award of Merit. In order to receive these awards, the cultivar needs to be distinctive, beautiful, and perform well over a wide geographic area. Although a professional horticulturist will systematically fertilize plants with special characteristics, traditional breeding can be more of a hit-or-miss proposition. When Edna Spaulding was asked how she bred three Stout Medal winners, she said, "Well, I just cross purty on purty." Her winning flowers were Luxury Lace, Lavender Flight, and Martha Adams.

So if you have an annoying bare spot in reasonable sunlight hurry out and ask a friend for some plants that you will enjoy next year!

Amaryllis Sparkles with Surprises

THESE PLANTS HAVE BECOME A FLAMBOYANT PART of the holiday season and cause perennial amazement at their size, color, and distinctive structures.

Over the years I have acquired a few of these plants and kept them on my windowsill. They always bloomed initially as advertised but, despite me following the instructions, they never bloomed again. Eventually I would throw them out and buy new ones. One day I went online and found a site that advised me to put them outdoors in their pot during the summer, occasionally watering them; bring them indoors as fall sets in; cut off the foliage; and expect new flowers. It worked for several years. Last year, nothing seemed to happen for weeks after I brought the pot indoors, and I planned to throw the bulb away. I pulled the entire plant out of the pot, saw all the tangled roots, which appeared pinkish and plump with water, and said, "These do not look dead to me." I replaced the bulb in the same pot and, shortly thereafter, saw new leaf growth and eventually the usual four magnificent red flowers.

Writing about daylilies, I discussed hand-pollinating flowers. Since the flower structures of the Amaryllis are so large and distinct and so similar to those of daylilies, I thought I would experiment and see if I could produce seed. Indeed, I could—the plant producing large, three-seamed capsules that eventually opened, exposing a multitude of seed. I planted a large number of them in the spring of 2016 and now I have six baby Amaryllis, although I am told it can take up to five years for the babies to mature to bloom size. If it didn't take so long from parent to seed to new bloom, I might have invested in several more bulbs of different colors to see what kinds of new colors and shapes I could produce.

The name Amaryllis derives from the Greek *amarysso*—"to sparkle." Greek mythology speaks of a young maiden, unsurprisingly named Amaryllis, who was in love with a disinterested youth named Alteo. Alteo's main interest was flowers, and he declared that he could only fall in love with a maiden who brought him a new, delightful bloom. The Delphic Oracle advised Amaryllis to prick herself and let the drops fall to the ground. Eventually, a large crimson flower grew from these drops and she, thereby, won his heart. The flower has come to symbolize pride, determination, and radiant beauty.

But nothing is ever simple when it comes to plants. It turns out that the plant that we all know as an Amaryllis —related to daffodils— is not an *Amaryllis* at all; in fact it is a *Hippeastrum,* and the true *Amaryllis* is an altogether different plant from the West Cape region of South Africa; ours is South American, found in tropical and sub-tropical areas from Argentina to Mexico. The German botanist Eduard Friedrich Poeppig (1798–1868) spent many years in Chile, where he discovered the *Hippeastrum* in 1828 growing on a hillside.

Let us examine each of these plants:

The true Amaryllis, known botanically as *Amaryllis belladonna* grows in zones 7–9. In theory, that means that we could actually try growing it outdoors in Riverdale, New York, which is listed as zone 7a, indicating that minimal winter temperatures here range from 0°–5°F. It is always amusing to test plant limits, and I might try one day growing them outdoors, although I would have to be prepared to lose them. The largely pink flowers are scented, and up to twelve blooms may grow on a single solid stem.

The unscented *Hippeastrum* grows in zones 9–11. They had already been brought to Europe in the eighteenth century and have been extensively hybridized. The bulb seems to grow best when crowded in its pot. It was named *Hippeastrum* by the Reverend William Herbert, a British botanist, botanical illustrator, and poet. In 1819 he separated the plants (the true *Amaryllis* and the *Hippeastrum*) into separate genera based on his own research; he is known for his book *Amaryllidaceae*, published in 1837. While my *Hippeastrum* only puts out four flowers, at 90° angles to each other on a hollow stem, the total possible number of flowers is fourteen.

Huge and Exotic, Elephant Ears Fascinate

WITH OUR IRRIGATION SYSTEM turned off and nighttime temperatures plummeting, it was time to clean up the hoses and watering cans until spring. It was also time to dig up some of the tender perennials that can't survive a New York winter. This past weekend I went around the garden and dug up those caladium bulbs that I could still locate.

My efforts, however, were focused particularly on the elephant ears. Generally, I try to avoid plants that require too much maintenance, but I am so taken with the size and the exotic quality of those plants that I cannot resist them. Still, the elephant ears must be dug up each fall, wrapped in newspaper, and put in a cool garage. Come April, I unwrap them and start them indoors, so that by the time the weather warms up enough, they will show some growth and can make a visual statement in the garden.

Several years ago, a friend was culling his elephant ears, *Colocasia esculenta*, and offered me one. It was huge and gorgeous, and I thought that I would overwinter it indoors so as to enjoy it during the cold weather as well, but the strangest thing kept happening. Every morning, I would find a puddle on the floor underneath one or another of the leaves. I assumed at first that I had inadvertently dripped water when watering. But after several occurrences, it was clear that I couldn't be that careless, so I started investigating. Apparently, some plants—including *Colocasia esculenta*, strawberry, and equisetum—can exude excess watery sap in a process called "guttation" first studied by Burgerstein in 1887. The cause is root pressure generated by excess water in the soil around the roots.

This was definitely not going to work on my wooden floors, so I gave the plant to a friend with tile floors and bought myself new tubers in the spring.

I first became acquainted with elephant ears through displays at various public gardens in which they were labeled *Colocasias*. But there were also very similar plants labeled *Alocasias*. And just to confuse the picture further, another similar group is called *Xanthosomas*.

A little digging clarified the situation somewhat. All three of these groups are member of the family *Aracea*, subdivided further into the subfamily *Aroideae*. Further, the *Colocasia* and the *Alocasia* are member of the tribe *Colocasiae*, while the *Xanthosomas* are from the *Caladieae*, which include the caladiums.

I always find the *Araceae* fascinating. We generally expect seeds to form within petalled flowers or fruit. But the *Aracea* —otherwise known as *aroids*—bear a flower stalk called a "spadix," partially wrapped in sheath called a "spathe." The Amorphophallus at the New York Botanical Garden that I wrote about earlier, and that had the local plant aficionados hyperexcited, is likewise an aroid. I always imagine these plants as benign cobras nestled in the greenery. Despite never having seen such an inflorescence on my elephant ears, I have found baby plants in unexpected places, attesting to their occurrence.

Whenever plants are placed into different groups, it is clear that there are substantial botanical differences between them. Let's look into some obvious differences—although I will completely ignore the issue of differences in flower morphology.

Colocasia: The heart-shaped leaves tend to droop downward with the stem attaching to the leaf, not at the edge (leaf notch), but set somewhat underneath the leaf. The corm—the swollen base of the stem from which new plants will grow—tends to be rounded. They like full sun and do well in wet soil.

Alocasia: The leaves, which are frequently shiny and have pointed tips, tend to point upward, and the corm is more elongated. They grow best in shade and well-drained soil. The leaves are attached by the petioles at the leaf notch on the edge of the leaf.

Xanthosomas: The leaves are arrow-shaped (sagittate), with a smooth, waxy upper surface and thick ribs on the lower surface. The leaves droop downward with the petiole attachment at the leaf notch.

Poi, a starchy Hawaiian food staple, is made from an edible taro of the *Colocasia* family. Most aroids, however, are toxic to humans, and it is not readily apparent how to detoxify them or identify edible varieties.

I may look into buying the large and architecturally exciting *Alocasia amazonica* to expand my repertoire with these plants.

Unpronounceable Beauty

LIVING IN RIVERDALE, NEW YORK, WE ARE SPOILED by our proximity to the New York Botanical Garden. It has 240 lush acres filled with flowers, extraordinary tree collections, specialty gardens, and regular exhibitions in the Conservatory. And for those of a more academic bent, it has a wonderful library filled with journals devoted to every conceivable botanical interest—among them paleobotany, desert plants, mosses, and bonsai. We travel to Israel frequently. However, we sometimes try to add variety by adding other destinations in a European city on the return trip. Several years ago, we chose London. Despite the fact that we had only about three days there, we managed to visit two botanical gardens. The smaller one is Chelsea Physic Garden on Hospital Road, which was established in 1673 as the Apothecaries' Garden to grow medicinal plants. Plants there are grown in two different groupings. The first is by botanical family, the second by usage—so, for example, those plants used for gastric disorders are all grown together.

But Kew Gardens—not to be confused with the neighborhood in Queens, New York—is an extraordinary botanical garden covering 326 acres on the outskirts of London. Although the garden was started as a private royal preserve in 1759, it was transformed by Sir Joseph Banks in 1772 into a center of botanical knowledge and scientific research focused on finding new plants for food and horticulture. I highly recommend the book *The Plant Hunters*, by T. Musgrave, C. Gardner and W. Musgrave, about these intrepid explorers.

We took a full day to explore the entire garden, and I must admit that, after about five hours, I could barely move. The first building that we explored was the Conservatory, arranged in row upon row of flowering plants from tropical locations. It always amazes me that plants, which presumably have no aesthetic sense—or do they?—have flowers of such extraordinary structural complexity and surprising coloration.

But today's story is primarily about scent. As I was walking down a particular aisle, the most extraordinary floral scent practically overpowered me. I retraced my steps several times in an effort to locate the responsible plant. As you know, your scent receptors wear out rapidly for a given scent, so it took several passes, with me sniffing each set of flowers, before I zeroed in on the right plant. It turned out that it has the unpronounceable name *Hedychium flavescens* (hed-*i*-kiyum fla-*ves*-ens) and is a member of the ginger family (*Zingiberaceae*). It is known colloquially as the cream garland-lily, yellow ginger or cream ginger. I decided then and there that I had to have one and, instead of saying to myself that I would remember the name, I actually wrote it down.

Returning to the U.S., I started making inquiries about buying the plant. Much to my surprise, almost no one seemed to have one, although many related gingers are easily available. After several Internet searches, I found one nursery in California (since closed) that did have some in stock. The proprietor said the plants were in dormancy but he would get back to me later in the season. After waiting a year and a half, I finally accepted the fact that this request had fallen through the cracks and called again. The owner apologized; within three weeks, I had a tuber and a list of instructions.

That summer I put it in the sunniest place I could find outdoors, and it grew to six feet and put out two sets of blooms that were worth sniffing. But I wasn't sure I could successfully overwinter the plant indoors.

Since I was volunteering then at the New York Botanical Garden, I asked if they would overwinter it in return for a cutting. A deal was struck, since they did not have that particular plant variety. At the end of the following summer, my *Hedychium* had grown well again. I divided the plant, kept the smallest piece for myself, and gave two back to NYBG as my gift, where, I understand, it is being appreciated. Incidentally, I did overwinter the plant in the brightest room in my house, and while it didn't flower during the winter, it remained in fine shape for the next summer season.

The Wondrously Varied Hosta

NATURE'S GIFT TO SHADE GARDENERS are ferns, astilbe, and hostas. I knew nothing about any of them when I first started gardening. In fact, I had no idea what the patch of well-shaped green plants growing in the back yard even was until years later. I was, however, very taken by their beautiful sculptured leaves—glossy and heart-shaped, with a beautiful vein pattern networked throughout.

In a fit of experimentation fever one day, I dug up a clump and discovered that it had a crown, which seemed dividable, together with little plantlets growing round the crown. Not one to let prudence hinder me, I started dividing all the clumps and planting the plantlets and the crown sections.

Eventually, I had so many hosta that I had to start giving some away. But that took many years, and in the meanwhile I came to realize that this is a wonderful family of plants that can not only handle shady conditions but comes in a veritable kaleidoscope of colors and textures.

They grow in various tones of green, blue, and yellow—and not merely monotonous single colors. There are all manner of variegations, with each cultivar showing slightly different swirls of white, cream, and yellow. The leaf textures run the gamut from smooth to puckered. The leaves can be heart-shaped, oval, or lanceolate. They can also drape downward or assume a cup shape. They can be huge when fully grown, forming clumps six feet across, or small, and never grow more than a few inches high. In short, there is a hosta for every taste and purpose.

There is also a hosta society, which, as I wrote earlier, indicates a high level of horticultural interest. In this case, it is the American Hosta Society, whose website contains information for all levels of interest. I was particularly interested in reading Steven C. Chamberlain's two articles on hybridizing. Although he is much more rigorous about controlling conditions than I ever was, carefully pollinating selected plants, and keeping meticulous records, hostas are easy to grow from seed.

The seed needs to be kept dry and cool though not necessarily refrigerated, and can just be scattered on moist sterile soil, placed under grow lights which can be kept on for the entire twenty-four hours, and green seedlings will pop up in just a few weeks. While I had fun seeing the new babies, I never had anything particularly unusual grow out for me.

Hostas are another non-native plant coming to us from Asia. Evidence exists that the plant originated in China about 15,000 years ago and then spread to Korea and Japan. The first hostas grown in Europe came from seeds of *Hosta plantaginea* sent in 1784 from China and planted in Jardin des Plantes in Paris, France. The first living plants—*Hosta ventricosa*—came in 1790, also from China. Then, in 1829, living plants came to Europe from Japan through the graces of Philipp von Siebold, a botanist and physician working for the Dutch East India Company and living on the island of Dejima in Nagasaki Harbor. With the exception of that trading-company colony, Japan was not open to the West until 1853, when Commodore Perry sailed into Nagasaki Harbor.

Since hostas were discovered and described by Europeans before the Linnaean system of categorizing plants with a Latin binomial system was widely used, the original botanical names were unlike those used today. However, an Austrian botanist in 1812, Leopold Trattinnick, grouped all these plants into the genus *Hosta* in honor of another Austrian botanist, Nicholas Thomas Host. There has been controversy over time as to the correct scientific placement of these plants. It was first classified as *Liliaceae*, then *Agavaceae*, and now it has its own unique family *Hostaceae*.

While the *H. plantaginea* that I had growing in my backyard is not the most flamboyant of the hostas available, it has one particularly great feature—its fragrant flowers. Hosta flowers appear on a long stalk called a scape, and most hosta varieties have scapes that support a multitude of small purple flowers. Those flowers have no scent. But *H. plantaginea* has a highly fragrant group of white flowers, although only one bloom per plant opens each day. They open in the evening and close up forever in the morning. If you are lucky enough to have a group of them, the enveloping perfume scents the evening air.

If you are blessed with too much shade, take comfort in knowing that, by using only those hosta varieties already available, you can create a true work of art.

La Vie En Rose

IMITATION," GOES THE OLD ADAGE, "is the sincerest form of flattery." The gardener's version of that is a request for plants and cuttings. Fortunately, ardent gardeners are generally eager to share favorite plants and information about their cultivation.

One late-spring day, I was visiting a friend in Riverdale, New

York, whose garden includes a steep hillside. As I drove up, I saw that the entire slope was covered with a silvery plant that had small magenta flowers, and I could immediately feel the plant-lust emerging! When I left, I was carrying several specimens. That prize turned out to be *Lychnis coronaria*—the rose campion.

The plant is not native to the United States; sources vary over whether it originated in southeastern Europe or North Africa, but it was already being grown in England in the 1600s. Thomas Jefferson, at age twenty-four, noted it growing at Shadwell, his boyhood home in Albemarle County, Virginia. Throughout his life, Jefferson was interested in natural history and kept extensive notes on his farms and gardens. On June 4, 1767, he wrote that the larkspur, poppies, and lychnis were in bloom. Jefferson was, you may recall, the president who signed the Louisiana Purchase and sent out the Lewis and Clarke Expedition, which kept extensive journals on their travels. These journals included 160 mentions of plants and nine of geology.

Generally, lychnis naturalize easily if they receive sufficient light and are not overwatered. However, I had not counted on their being biennials—which means that I was looking at two years from seed to flower.

There are essentially three life-cycle patterns for herbaceous plants - those that do not have woody stems and that die back completely at the end of the growing season.

The first type are annuals, which we buy each year at a nursery for summer color and which live out their lives in one season. There are some crops that we grow in our northern gardens as annuals but that actually are perennials when grown in their warmer native climates. These include petunias, geranium, tomatoes, and peppers.

The second possible life cycle is that of the perennials. Here the plants are long-lived. While it can take a few years for the plant to produce its first flowers and set seed, perennials do not wither and die away completely. The following spring will see new growth, and the plant will go through another growing-season cycle including flowers and seed. I cannot expend the yearly energy necessary for annuals, so my garden is chock full of perennials such as hosta (genus *Hosta*), astilbe (Genus *Astilbe*), cranesbill (*Geranium maculatum*), and Joe Pye weed (Genus *Eupatorium*), and various genera of lilies.

There is, however, one caveat regarding the perennial category. Some perennials are relatively fragile and are grown as biennials. Hollyhocks, for example, seem susceptible to rust diseases by their second year and therefore are routinely removed from the garden at the end of the second growing season.

Which leads us to the third category, that of biennials: In this case, the plant only puts out foliage the first year, very often in the shape of a rosette. Only during the second growing season does flowering occur, seed set, and the mother plant dies, hopefully to be replaced by her numerous seedlings the following spring. Common biennial flowers include foxglove, which gives us digitalis and Canterbury bells. Some of our common vegetable crops are actually biennial, but we harvest them in the first season. Those include cabbage, kale, brussel sprouts, carrots, and celery.

The genus name Lychnis seems to come from the Greek *lychnis,* meaning "lamp." The ancients may have used the wooly leaves as lamp wicks. *Coronaria* refers to garlands or crowns and may have indicated that they were considered fit for a victor's garland in athletic games.

Lychnis is part of *the Caryophyllaceae* family, which includes carnations, baby's breath, and the annoying chickweed. In addition to the attractive flowers, which can also be white, I am enamored of the silver foliage, which "pops" the colors of darker surrounding plants.

Some other popular plants for brightening shadier garden areas include the Japanese painted fern, 'Silver Shimmers' pulmonaria, 'Jack Frost' brunnera, and Dusty Miller (*Senecio cineraria*). Other plants with interesting felted and hairy leaves are lamb's ear (*Stachys byzantine*), wooly thyme (*Thymus pseudolanuginosus*) and ornamental mullein (*Verbascum*).

Finally, I have numerous flowering lychnis all over the garden, which augers well for future seasons.

Beware the Treacherous Cactus

CACTUS FRUIT IS NOW regularly available in stores. With its dark rose-colored peel, and similarly colored pulp filled with hard black seeds, it is very refreshing served chilled during the summer. It certainly seems innocuous enough piled on grocery shelves. But if you have ever considered foraging these fruits in the wild, think very carefully!

My introduction to cactus fruit came many years ago while vacationing in Israel, when we spent a few days in a tourist cottage in the vegetarian village of Amirim. The only request made of guests was that no meat products should be prepared using the utensils provided by the cottage owners.

The cottages were single-family units, each meticulously landscaped with a variety of plants, including mature *Opuntia* specimens standing over five feet tall.

My general policy around spiny plants is to use extreme caution. However, the *Opuntia* did not strike me as particularly problematic, since I could see my supermarket fruit growing atop many of the plants. The perfect analogy here is to expect real panda bears to be as cuddly as a teddy bear.

I was standing outside as another guest in an adjacent driveway guest was directing a car backing up into that driveway. As the car rolled back, the man stepped back too, right into a large *Opuntia*. He yelped and jumped forward, and I assumed that, except for a few painful pricks, he would be just fine. How foolish of me!

While *Opuntia* do have spines, they are not very long. The real menace, however, comes from the *Opuntia's* small hair-like structures called "glochids." They grow in tufts, and there are numerous glochids in each tuft. To think of them simply as little hairs is to do them a terrible injustice. It would be like calling a poison ivy rash just a skin inflammation! Glochids break off, lodge in the skin, and cause unbearable irritation. They are so fine that it can take days to pull them all out manually, assuming you can actually see them clearly. At moments like that, nearsightedness is a real advantage.

Seeing the man was in agony, I wondered how the fruit could be safely picked. There are a few simple rules. Never pick fruit on a windy day, always wear heavy gloves, and after you pick it, roll the fruit thoroughly in the dirt to remove the glochids.

I have been a volunteer for a long time at the New York Botanical Garden, in which one of the collection rooms is devoted entirely to cacti and succulents, both categories primarily adapted to warm climates with dry conditions.

Cacti, with one exception, are New World plants; succulents can be found growing on almost every continent. The distinguishing characteristic of a cactus are small, round cushion-like structures called "areoles." It is from these areoles that the spines, branches, glochids, and flowers grow. Fortunately, the only sub-family containing glochids are the *Opuntioideae*.

I had never been particularly interested in cacti or succulents. But I have a good friend who has restricted herself to growing them as houseplants because she travels and these plants do well without watering for several weeks. As I became more familiar with them, I began to admire their shapes and varied growth habits. Their most remarkable aspect is the fabulous flowers many of them produce, as if to make up for the structural toughness they display the balance of the year.

Recently I was grooming the collection in the succulent house. In the second row, there was a small *Opuntia* with the most gorgeous, fuzzy new growth of cinnamon-colored areoles. Knowing better, I certainly did not intend to touch it with my bare hands. However, as I reached across it to pick up a plant in the row behind it, I felt something prickling me. I looked down to see that the back of my hand looked as if it had been dipped in cinnamon. Fortunately, with a pair of small tweezers used for grooming, I was able to pluck out most of the glochids in less than an hour. It was suggested later that I might also try some form of sticky tape to pull them off *en masse* in the event of a future encounter.

Plants are the basis for all animal life, but they are not defenseless. They have evolved numerous strategies to protect themselves.

Peonies, Flowers of the Gods

BUYING A HOUSE ISN'T MERELY about buying a building. The property that comes with it is ripe with options. Large trees anchor the property, while perennials offer suggestions. When we bought our home many years ago, there were clumps of plants I could not identify in various locations.

One clump, stuck in a shady spot way out of the way, simply put out leaves each spring and left it at that. Eventually, I learned that they were peonies. I was never clear why they didn't bloom in the old location—maybe they didn't have enough sun, or the roots were buried too deeply—but one fall I got around to moving them to the front border, and the yearly wait until they bloom is definitely worth it.

This year they were in full bloom just in time for the Shavuot holiday in early June, and three cut blossoms perfumed the entire dining room.

All peonies are members of the genus *Paeonia* and are the only members of the family *Paeoniaceae*. This family is part of Order *Saxifragales*, which makes peonies a distant cousin to coral bells, astilbes, and tiarellas. There are about thirty-three known species in all, the majority being herbaceous, the remainder woody, shrub forms. They are native to cold-temperate parts of Asia, Europe, and Western North America. The name derives from the Greek *Paeon*, physician of the gods, who we know as Apollo. Despite appearing in the traditional medicine of various cultures, the entire plant is actually considered poisonous.

And yes, there is a society—the American Peony Society (APS)— dedicated to the promotion of cultivated peonies and their improvement as garden plants. Formed in 1903, its first task was to standardize the naming of various cultivars, and since 1974 the APS has served as the International Cultivar Registration Authority. Despite the fact that the peony may once have had as few as five petals, it is now a large and densely petalled flower. At present the APS categorizes herbaceous peonies into five classes in addition to the "Single" type, which represents the basic structure. The others forms are Japanese, Anemone, Bomb, Double, and Semi-Double.

Like many flowers, peonies have both male and female reproductive structures on the same flower—the male structures are the stamens, the female the pistils. The species peony is self-fertile but crosses easily with nearby peony plants. The various different peony flower categories are the result of transformations of some of the stamens into petal-like structures.

Those plants in the Japanese classification have stamens that are still recognizable although hugely increased in size and number, usually yellow and somewhat lumpy. As these staminodes transform further into a petal-like structures, they are called Anemones, with a "center ball of contrasting size resting on a flat or cupped saucer-shape" formed by the outer petals, called the "guard" petals. The Bomb category sees a complete transformation of the stamens into petals, with a center snowball overshadowing the outer petals.

The remaining forms are the Double and the Semi-Double. A Double is essentially a complete flower within a flower. Finally, if stamens are visible in the opened Double flower, it becomes a Semi-Double.

For anyone who wants to try their hand at growing peonies, the seeds are doubly dormant and need to undergo two chilling periods separated by a warm period. After the first chilling, the seed puts out roots only, with stems and leaves appearing after the second chilling.

In addition to the herbaceous form, there is also a tree peony (*Paeonia suffruticosa*) which can reach a height of 3 to 5 feet. Known as the 'King of Flowers' in the Tang Dynasty (618–906 C.E.), it was the symbol of happiness, richness, and prosperity. By the Song Dynasty (960 C.E.), there were over 200 described cultivars. In 1798, the first tree peony was introduced into Europe and was planted at Kew Gardens in London.

Based on genetic studies, the tree peony seems to be a natural hybrid arising from the crossing of just a few peony species. *Paeonia cathayana* seems to be the maternal parent, with only a small number of peony species acting as the male parent.

Finally there are the Itoh peonies, created in 1948 by Toichi Itoh, also called "intersectional peonies." These were created by using pollen from the tree peony "Alice Harding" to fertilize the herbaceous *Paeonia lactiflora* "Katoden." These plants flower longer and on stronger stems than the typical herbaceous plants, and are likely to be the future of cultivated peonies.

While the Itoh cultivars are a bit pricey, I think one is probably in my future.

A Smelly but Welcome Winter Plant: Skunk Cabbage

THEY DON'T CALL IT skunk cabbage for nothing! I still remember being warned off the plant as a youngster. While it seemed to me then to have only a heavy oniony smell, many compare it to the smell of skunk or rotting meat. Calling to mind also the Amorphophallus at the New York Botanical Garden, you might wonder if there is a whole world of plants with terrible scents pollinated by flies.

The scientific name for our American native skunk cabbage is *Symplocarpus foetidus,* the latter word being Latin for "fetid"—"having a heavy and offensive odor." Other plants where *foetidus* is part of the scientific name include *Helleborus foetidus,* the spice asafetida (*Fer-*

ula assafoetida), and the Persian yellow rose (*Rosa foetida*). Other fly-pollinated plants include the paw-paw tree (*Asimina triloba*) and the red trillium (*Trillium erectum*). And we must also thank midges for pollinating cacao trees (*Theobroma cacao*), without whose stalwart efforts chocolate would never pass our lips.

Immediately at the Jackson Avenue entrance to Sprain Ridge Park in Yonkers (New York), there is a boggy area and, poking through the muddy water, around late January /early February one can spot small curved dark green spathes speckled with purple. Because of the ooze, one can't, and probably shouldn't, walk near them, but a long lens on a camera is a wonderful thing. Intigued, I persevered, and I finally found the plant popping up all over.

Skunk cabbage relies on several different insects for pollination—scavenging flies, stoneflies (which seem to spend their lifecycle near water), and bees. . .even in cold weather. Winter stoneflies actually emerge and reproduce during the fall and height of winter.

How does a plant form leaves and fruiting structures when the weather is so cold? In this case, the leaf cones and presumptive flowering structures are formed in the summer and lie within the crown of the plant, waiting for the days to start lengthening again. Like the *Amorphophallus* the female structures grow higher on the spadix than the pollen-producing anthers, and they mature earlier, so self-fertilization is generally avoided. Seeds form and fall in the vicinity of the mother plant, where they will later grow into new babies.

Skunk cabbage foliage provides food for the *Phragmatobia fuliginosa* caterpillars, the ruby tiger moth. Later in the season these larvae will feed on dock, goldenrod, Joe-Pye weed, as well as other plants. This moth is found throughout the northern United States, and the adults can be seen from April through October. Most animals avoid eating the leaves of skunk cabbage, though, because they contain irritating calcium oxalate crystals.

There is also another native species of western skunk cabbage—*Lysichiton americanus*—growing from Wyoming to the Pacific. It was introduced as a bog plant into the United Kingdom in 1901 and has since become naturalized in both England and Ireland.

Like the *Amorphophallus*, skunk cabbage is an arum of the family *Araceae*. These are the jack-in-the-box plants with a cobra-like hood (spathe) surrounding the flowering stalk (spadix). Many articles say that flowering is accompanied by a noticeable smelliness.

Skunk cabbage has two other fascinating features: contractile roots, and thermogenesis. "Contractile roots" mean exactly what the terms suggests. The roots are usually plump and fleshy, and actually pull the plant crown deeper into the mud with each passing year, so that it is practically impossible to remove a plant completely from its bed.

"Thermogenesis" means raising body temperature above the temperature of the ambient air. This is one of the adaptations usually associated with warm-blooded animals. While not unique to skunk cabbage, it is unusual in plants. Two other plants that can create their own heat are *Philodendrum selloum* and *Nelumbo nucifera*. Thermogenesis in plants usually lasts only a few hours or at most a few days, but skunk cabbage can maintain a temperature of 59–71°F. for over two weeks while the ambient temperature is 5–50°F. The purpose of this warmth may be to vaporize the flower scent in order to attract pollinators to the protected hollow created by the surrounding spathe.

So winter may not be a gardening season, but Nature is never asleep. There is more going on around us than we ever imagined!

The Snake Plant Otherwise Known as Mother-in-Law's Tongue

EW PEOPLE ARE FOND OF SNAKES. Mothers-in-law and their tongues also have a poor reputation. Attitudes towards either have not changed much over time.

However, personal preferences can and do evolve. A photo essay in the *New York Times Magazine* contained portraits taken on successive birthdays. It was intriguing to watch faces morph with age and experience.

Plant appreciation can also undergo a natural evolution. When I began gardening, I wanted swaths of colorful blooms. Nature herself quickly disabused me of that idea. Color requires intense sunshine, but we had been blessed with large, beautiful trees which create shade. Nature, who certainly abhors a vacuum, introduced me to the amazing variety of shade plants.

How do the *Sansevieras* (snake plants) relate to evolving tastes? My general distaste for them may have resulted from seeing far too many of these bedraggled plants in medical offices. Usually just plunked down on tabletops in a vain effort to create a homey atmosphere, the plants plainly suffered from low light and poor watering.

While in Co-op City (a Bronx neighborhood) several years ago, I entered the sunny lobby of a tall apartment building. Large planters wrapped around two sides of the lobby, filled with ranks of *Sansevieras* of differing sizes and colors. Until that moment I had never seen any other than the mottled variety with gray-green, leathery, lance-like leaves. The lobby specimens were much more varied and exciting. Some were green, some mottled. Some had yellow borders and yellow streaking, others had white streaking and white borders. Some even had cylindrical leaves. All in all, the scene evoked wonder for a plant I would not have considered buying ten minutes earlier.

Investigating these plants a little further, I was startled to find out that they are related to our edible vegetable the asparagus, both being members of the monocot family *Asparagaceae*. Briefly, as these seeds germinate and send out their first true leaves, they have only a single leaf in contrast to dicots, which put out two leaves. The bulk of our familiar plants are, in fact, dicots, so a monocot always catches my attention. Other monocots include grasses, palms, bananas, and lilies.

Knowing that you can buy white and green asparagus, I was curious if they were different species. In fact, they are the same plant, the white version being achieved by preventing the plant stalks from photosynthesizing and thereby turning green. This is accomplished by mounding soil over the asparagus stem as it emerges from the soil.

Propagating plants is always fun, although there's usually a trade-off between time and money. The leathery versions of the *Sansevieria* can be propagated in two ways. The easiest is to separate offsets—basically baby plants—that emerge at the base of an established plant. When the offset seems substantial enough, you can remove the entire plant from the pot, tease out the babies and repot mommy and babies separately.

The other method is to make leaf cuttings. Take a long leaf and cut it into three-inch sections, remembering to keep each section oriented in the growing position. Using a moist potting medium of half sand and half peat, firmed down, insert the cutting with the bottom part wedged into the soil, and cover the pot with a clear plastic bag to maintain a moist environment. Care must be taken that the bag does not touch the cuttings. *Sansevieria* cuttings, however, create new plants only from the center of the leaf cutting, so a plant with variegation along the edge will yield a totally green plant. To propagate variegated plants, one must use offsets.

I was startled once to see a *Sanseviera* in bloom and it should not be missed!

Strobilanthes' Beautiful Relatives

STROLLING PAST ONE OF MY FAVORITE PLANTS, a Strobilanthes which is not well known in these parts, I thought I would devote my column solely to it. A little research informed me, however, that Strobilanthes is part of the *Acanthaceae* family, which includes another favorite of mine, bear's breeches or acanthus. I decided the combination was too good to miss.

There are many choice foliage plants for summer, but coleus with its tremendous range of fancy leaf patterns and colors, is the most common.

When I spotted my first Strobilanthes in a public garden, I knew I had to try it. The leaves are ovaloid. The upper surface is dark green, with silvery iridescent pink-purple markings radiating from the central vein while the underside is purple. Its common name is Persian shield perhaps invoking ancient Persian military shields that could actually be either oval or round. Personally, the Strobilanthes shape reminds me more of Zulu shields.

Strobilanthes, native to Myanmar, is a genus of 350 species with some species cultivated for their hooded flowers growing in shades of blue, pink, white, and purple. However, the species most likely to be seen locally in cultivation is *Strobilanthes dyeriana*, and its attraction is clearly the leaves.

The name *Strobilanthes* derives from the Greek *strobilus*, meaning "cone," and *anthos,* meaning "flower," since that is the shape of the flower in some *Strobilanthes* species. The second part of the Latin name, in this case *dyeriana,* is known as the "epithet." In this case, the name was bestowed in honor of Sir William Turner Thiselton-Dyer, director of the Royal Botanic Garden in Kew, England, from 1885 to 1905. With an eye to the economic development of British colonies, he introduced rubber plantations to Sri Lanka and Malaysia as well as cacao plantations to Sri Lanka.

While *Strobilanthes* is winter hardy in zones 10–11 and can grow to four feet in these warmer climates, it can only be grown as an annual in this area and will be shorter. It can be overwintered as a houseplant and propagated through cuttings in the spring. As the mother plant ages, however, it develops a woodier stem and the foliage quality from these cuttings declines. Late summer cuttings are suggested instead for overwintering. The hardest part about growing them in the Northeast is locating them at a local nursery.

The first time I saw the next plant I want to discuss, we were on a springtime trip in Israel. It seemed to be growing throughout Jerusalem, but I didn't recognize it at all. There was a stalk covered with curved flowers, in lavender and white, resembling large snapdragon flowers, and no one I asked was able to shed light on its identity.

Eventually, I spotted one back in the States and discovered it was either an *Acanthus mollis* or *Acanthus spinosus,* desirable for its large, architectural foliage as well as its flowered stalk. The name *acanthus* derives from the Greek *acanthi,* meaning "spiny" and referring to the thorny edges on some species. The theme is continued with *spinosus* also referring to spines. The common name "bear's breeches" may be a corruption of the medieval nomenclature, which translates to "cultivated spiny bear bract" ("resembling a bear claw"), with "bract" becoming corrupted to "breech(es)".

It grows as evergreen clumps through zone 7 and spreads by underground runners and can be propagated by root cuttings. Apparently, it can be hard to control in warmer climates, which does not explain why I lost the only one I ever tried growing. It seems to prefer partial shade and a moist soil, which can sometimes be hard to achieve in our hot August weather.

Designs derived from the large acanthus leaves have been used as ornamental motifs in architecture, most notably in the Corinthian columns of the ancient Greeks. They were also used by the Romans, and in Byzantine and medieval structures, and still appear in modern buildings.

As houseguests on a recent trip to Richmond (Virginia), I wanted to bring a gift to our hosts. I decided that a plant for their garden would be most appreciated. Having spent the night in Williamsburg, Virginia, we ended up at a beautiful nursery, Forest Lane Botanicals. I asked the owner, Alan Wubbels, what was new and exciting among his plants. He instantly pointed out a variegated *Acanthus mollis*, "Tasmanian angel." If we had been returning home shortly, I would definitely have bought a second one for my own garden.

The Welwitschia Mirabilis, a Truly Remarkable Plant

I HAVE NEVER BEEN TO NAMIBIA and never expected to regret it. Over the years, however, *Welwitschia mirabilis* has cropped up in articles and classes as a supremely unique plant. Imagine my surprise when, wandering through the extensive tropical house at the Botanical Garden in Frankfurt (Germany), I saw a huge specimen through the glass walls. I stood there in shock and finally reached for the door knob, only to find that the room was locked. Apparently, it is only open to the public for a few hours once a week—and Friday, when we showed up, was not that day. Acknowledging intense public interest, there is a viewing gallery on the second floor together with a lengthy explanation of the plant's characteristics written, unfortunately for me, only in German and forcing me to do my research back in the States.

It is somewhat difficult to define the allure of *Welwitschia mirabilis*. Growing under severe conditions in the Namib Desert, which runs north along the Atlantic coast from Namibia into Angola, it has the rugged appearance of many desert plants. Considered a dwarf tree or shrub, it has a fibrous stem in the shape of an inverted cone (obconical) which reaches an average height of twenty inches, although one living specimen has reached six feet. The inverted cone is the result of the early death of the more-common growing point located at the top of the stem, forcing additional growth of the plant to come from the bottom. The twisted mass of leathery, strap-shaped leaves is, in reality, only two long leaves that grow continuously for the life of the plant. Weathering causes the ends of the these leaves to fray, lending the plant a tattered appearance. This tattering may be partially responsible for preventing the leaves from spreading outward, instead causing them to twist back toward the stem. Unfurled, they can reach up to forty-six feet in length.

Some theorize that these leaves act to shade the soil underneath the plant, slowing water evaporation and protecting the root system, which consists of a taproot together with some lateral roots. Insects and animals also find refuge in this shade.

The leaves have stomata (openings) on both sides (amphistomatic). Generally, stomata regulate gas exchange and allow for the evaporation of water. There is a recurring assumption with *Welwitschia* that the water droplets that condense onto the leaves from the nightly local fog—the result of a cold Atlantic Ocean current—are absorbed through the upper stomata, but this has not been proven. However, the water condensate on the leaves does roll down the leaves towards the stem and drips onto the soil, where it is absorbed by the taproot.

Welwitschia is "dioecious," meaning that there are male and female plants. The specialized branches producing the strobili—the beautiful conical structures containing the ovules and the pollen—grow upright from the stem, near the leaf bases. The salmon-colored cones are males, and the larger blue-green cones are female.

There is, also, a debate about how pollination occurs. Since the plant does not produce the huge amounts of pollen expected of a wind-pollinated plant and several insects are routinely seen on and around it, the present assumption is that *Welwitschia* is pollinated either by the beetle *Odontopus sexapunctatus* and/or by bees and wasps.

Another cause for the wonderment surrounding the *Welwitschia* is its extended life span. While the average seems to be 500 - 600 years, it is believed that some plants are between 1,500 and 2,000 years old. Fossil evidence can date the plant back 113 million years.

Mirabilis means "wonderful" in Latin. However, *Welwitschia* is not a name that just rolls off the tongue. It was chosen to honor the Austrian botanist Friedrich Welwitsch (1806–1872), who did most of his work in Portugal and the Portuguese colony of Angola. In 1859, he discovered our eponymous plant, which he named *Tumboa strobilifera*. It was renamed *Welwitschia* by Joseph Dalton Hooker, the director of the Royal Botanical Garden at Kew. In addition to this honor, six genera and 300 other species of plants are also named for Friedrich Welwitsch.

In 1861, Welwitsch returned to Portugal but then, with Portuguese permission, took his collections, amounting to thousands of specimens, to the British Museum and Kew Gardens. After his death, lawsuits between the Portuguese and the British were pursued over who would receive the best of the specimens.

Our *Welwitschia mirabilis* is the only member of the family *Welwitschiaceae*, in the division *Gnetophyta*. So whether you are amazed by its hardiness, its lifespan, or its unique growth patterns, this is a plant well worth knowing!

Water in the Garden

IN EARLY AUGUST, MY GARDEN starts sliding into fall. The weather is usually hot and very dry, and the plants look exhausted. With the advent of September, I start clearing away some of the paraphernalia that will not be needed until next summer.

Recently, I was scrubbing out a child's wading pool. Since everyone in the family has outgrown wading pools, it's a fair question why it has not been given away. But like other "stuff" I have held onto, I finally had use for it.

As birders will tell you, having drinking water available is essential for any garden catering to wildlife and should be included in any garden design. The fact that I find cats—who prey on songbirds and whom I would like to dissuade from visiting my garden—drinking the water also is a problem I have not yet solved.

The water itself poses a separate problem. Mosquitoes breed in standing water, and everyone is rightfully concerned these days about the West Nile and Zika viruses. In years past, although I never kept records on how long it took mosquito larvae to hatch, I have seen wrigglers swimming in such basins. That problem, at least, can be solved by sprinkling "Mosquito Bits" onto any watery surface in the garden. The "Bits" contain BTI, which stands for *Bacillus thuringiensis israelensis*. The original formulation of *Bacillus thuringiensis* was used as an environmentally safe pesticide against caterpillars. However, the subspecies *israelensis*, contained in the "Bits," was discovered in dead mosquito larvae in Israel in 1976 by two scientists, Goldberg and Margalit. It is effective against the larvae of mosquitoes, blackfly, and fungus gnats. BTI is completely safe around all other organisms, including people and their pets, since it acts solely on the intestines of the targeted larvae.

Learning about the susceptibility of fungus gnats to BTI was important for another reason. Some time ago, I managed to bring home a plant apparently growing in infested soil, and had been trying to get rid of those gnats ever since. So far I had only been using the "Bits" in standing water, but I think I will try sprinkling them around all my other houseplants as well.

When we moved into our home, there was a small reflecting pool in the backyard. With young children in the family, the first thing I did was fill it in, to prevent accidents.

But water plants enchant me. Wandering around a local Home Depot that spring, I came upon a boxed water lily root that was calling out to me. I had no clear idea of exactly how I would grow it, but I figured that, once I it was in the house, something would occur to me.

Once home, I remembered the wading pool. I dragged it out, filled it about five inches deep, and opened the container to find a small, dark, rough-looking root in a net bag. Since no instructions were included, I dropped it into the pool and figured Nature would take care of things.

The next morning, I went outside to see if anything was happening and found the root lying on the ground, outside the pool. I returned it to the water and found it on the ground again the following morning. Clearly, I had to protect it from whatever animals or birds were visiting the pool at night.

I brought the root indoors, put it in the largest glass vase I could find, which I filled with water. Over the next few days, I saw roots developing and small leaves pushing up on elongating stems that unrolled into tiny lily pads. Finally, when it had outgrown its container, I returned it to the pool and waited. Occasionally, I would find the whole mass on the ground, though there was no evidence of any animal nibbling on it. I waited the whole summer and never once saw a bloom.

While I blame low light for all my growing problems, it seems that I may have myself to blame. Finally checking for instructions online, I discovered that the root should have been potted in soil before being sunk into the pool.

The best part about discovering that you have made a serious gardening error is knowing that you have the opportunity to try again. Maybe this time, I'll have the fabulous blooms I've been looking for!

Winter Aconite: A Sudden Flash of Yellow

IT WAS ONE OF THOSE WINTER DAYS in 2017 that we all long for, when the temperature rose into the sixties, and I was by no means the only one in shirtsleeves. The snow from a recent storm had finally melted and I felt an almost primal urge to get out into the garden and do something.

One thing led to another, and I was soon filling up one garbage can after another with twigs and branches—thank you, New York City, for instituting organic recycling—and started cutting down flower stalks denuded of seeds and therefore of no further use to the local birds. This was so much more fun than housework!

As I disturbed patches of wet leaves layered over the flower beds, I found plants that I had not noticed for months. I found parsley and strawberry plants, and lamiastrum. Daffodils were also making an appearance, their leaves pushing up out of the soil.

As I continued to work, I beheld a sudden flash of yellow. My first reaction was that another piece of brightly colored trash, of which I seem to have an abundance, had blown into the yard and had been pinned down under the wet leaves. But as I reached for it, I was stunned to see that I had two beautiful winter aconite blooming away, and a great day became perfect!

Given its early flowering timetable, it is not surprising that the scientific name, *Eranthis hyemalis*, should aptly reflect that fact. The genus name *Eranthis* is the combination of two Greek words—*er* for "spring," and *anthos* for "flower." The species name, *hyemalis*, is from the Latin meaning "winter-flowering," which, together with the genus name, is perfect.

We tend to associate flowering solely with heat and bright sunlight. However, there is a serious strategy behind the early blooming of our spring plants. By doing so, before the deciduous trees begin to leaf out again, maximum light is available for plants growing beneath the trees. This light will diminish greatly as the season progresses.

I must admit that it is unlikely I will find any more winter aconite despite having planted bulbs several times over the years. The dark tuber is quite small and flat, and I—along with others— have had difficulty deciding which side should be planted up. I know I am not the only one that is confused, because instructions say that, if you have difficulty with orientation, the tuber should be planted on its side so that the root can easily grow downward and the stem upward.

Some say that planting waxed tubers helps, since the waxing keeps the tubers fresh. Another suggestion recommends a thorough soaking before planting, which presumably accomplishes the same thing. Many gardeners, however, instead suggest that it is best to ask a fellow gardener with a robust patch for some plants after blooming has finished. And another option would be to collect seed and scatter it around. Once a patch is established in appropriate conditions— woodland soil with deciduous shade—the plant will naturalize quite easily by bulb offsets called bulbils. To see such a marvel, Ithan Valley Park outside Philadelphia (PA) has an amazing show of hillsides covered in winter aconite in February and March.

Eranthis hyemalis is a member of the buttercup family –*Ranunculaceae*. The name derives from the Latin *Rana*, meaning "frog," and *Ranunculus*, meaning "little frog." The best explanation for the family name that I could find suggests that, since many members of the *Ranunculaceae*, like moist conditions, they are like "little frogs." The plants are native to western Europe and the Balkans, and have naturalized widely . *Ranunculaceae* seem to have developed in the Cretaceous Period, which began 145 MYA.

Many other members of the *Ranunculaceae* are familiar to the public. They include the hellebores (the Lenten rose); aquilegia, commonly known as columbine, with its four-chambered flower; clematis, a vine with outrageously large and brightly colored flowers; delphiniums; and the wildly poisonous aconitum or "monkshood," to just name a few.

Anyone out there willing to donate some plants, I have just the spot!

Trees & Shrubs

Ancient Trees in Israel

I T STARTED WITH A SWING through the bookshop at the New York Botanical Garden. I consider browsing in a bookstore a special treat and have been known to cancel trips in order not to miss a used-book sale. Moseying about to see what was new and interesting in botanical art books, I came across Beth Moon's *Ancient Trees: Portraits of Time*. Filled with exquisite black-and-white photographs of huge, twisted, and textured trees of great age from countries all around the globe, it included one particularly intriguing photo—an olive tree from Mahgar, a Druze village in Israel northwest of the Sea of Galilee.

That photo provided the impetus for an adventure. I assumed there must be more than one tree worth seeing during our forthcoming trip to Israel, and I did not feel like traveling all the way north to Mahgar.

When I came across a 2008 book entitled *101 Special and Amazing Trees in Israel* by Yaakov Shkolnik, with photographs by Hanan Isachar, I knew I could find something interesting closer to Jerusalem.

The book was published in cooperation with Keren Kayemet LeYisrael, better known in the States as the Jewish National Fund (JNF). Founded in 1901, the non-profit JNF was created to buy and develop land in present-day Israel. Since its founding, the organization has planted 240 million trees, built more than 230 dams and reservoirs, and established more than 1,000 parks.

Since I could not lay my hands on a copy of the book itself, I decided to try to contact Yaakov Shkolnik directly. He very graciously agreed to meet us at a café in Petach Tikvah, a substantial city filled with new apartment buildings about an hour's drive outside Jerusalem. He brought his only copy of the book along, and I discovered that, despite its English title, it was written in Hebrew. While I can manage to read Hebrew with some understanding, I prefer English; but I was delighted to glean some of the book's highlights during our conversation.

If ever anyone was destined to write a particular book, Yaakov's life drew a straight line to this one. During high school, he volunteered at the Field School for the Society for Protection of Nature in Israel (SPNI) at the Ein Gedi National Park. He later worked in the apple orchards of Kibbutz Malkiyah and studied agriculture and botany at Hebrew University. He then became a tour guide for SPNI—whose tours, incidentally, I highly recommend. He was an editor of *Eretz* magazine, a Hebrew language natural science publication (there is also an English version) and finally worked as a tour guide and freelance writer for JNF.

The genesis of the tree book occurred in 2003. Yaakov had written a short guidebook for the JNF listing eighteen spectacular and ancient trees, and public demand for the book was overwhelming, with 50,000 copies distributed. Once Moshe Gilad, editor at the publishing house Am Oved, realized the extent of public interest, he convinced Yaakov to do the text, contacted Hanan Isachar to do the photography, and voila—the book!

The color photographs speak for themselves, but Yaakov likes to tell the "stories of the trees." To demonstrate, he took us to see an enormous *Eucalyptus citriodora* planted as a street tree outside an apartment building at 8 Shapira Street, right there in Petach Tikvah.

Eucalyptus trees were imported to Israel to combat the malarial swamps, but the *E. citriodora* is a rare and unique specimen. The trunk sheds its bark yearly and is, therefore, smooth, with a silky appearance. The tree, meanwhile, has grown so tall, and is so old, that it is trussed by three cables twined through the branches. The *citriodora* epithet refers to the enticing lemony scent released when the stiff, leathery leaves are crushed. Some say that a lemony tea can be brewed from these leaves.

After thanking Yaakov, we drove off to Kibbutz Zova in the Judean Hills west of Jerusalem to see two more spectacularly gnarled trees featured in his book. Within a few steps of each other stand an ancient olive tree (*Olea europaea*) and a Kermes oak (*Quercus calliprinos*). Traditionally, the branches of olive trees are heavily pruned, while the trunks continue to grown and thicken. Although this tree has a massive but hollow trunk, it continues sprouting masses of leaves.

The Kermes Oak as it usually exists in Nature is scarcely more than a shrub. This specimen, however, has a huge trunk requiring three supporting poles to keep it upright.

A little googling will yield other fabulous trees worth a visit on your next trip to Israel.

Golden Forsythia

F OR MOST OF THE YEAR forsythias are just a scruffy, lanky bush but its charms in the early spring amply justify its place in so many gardens. As part of the great spring sweep of yellow, I await its blooming to surround me with its golden splendor. However, as I watched bush after bush bloom in 2017, I was very disappointed, by the sparseness of the flowers. And those flowers that did bloom seemed concentrated at the branch tips instead of enveloping the shrub from top to bottom . Since much of my gardening is done by the seat of my pants, I started reading to see what needed to be done to improve matters.

Not terribly surprising, it seems that forsythia—like so many other bushes—require thoughtful pruning. They do not have a dominant trunk; the plant just puts up new canes during the growing season and next year's buds are set during the late summer. Professional advice suggests that a forsythia which is blooming poorly despite adequate sunlight, be pruned back about 1/3 before late summer, by cutting the older, thicker canes down to the soil line.

However, all was not lost that spring. Forsythia branches can be easily forced—blooming indoors weeks before they bloom outdoors. About six weeks before outdoor bloom time, I decided that I had had enough of winter. The weather was yo-yoing up and down, just teasing us. I finally decided that I would brighten up the indoors even if the outdoors was uncooperative. I went outside and cut a half a dozen heavily budded forsythia branches and put them in tepid water in a window receiving afternoon light. Not five days later, all the buds had opened and the room was transformed.

Although I have never tried forcing any other tree branches, good candidates—which must be woody and deciduous—include dogwood, pussy willow, and fothergilla. Apparently all you have to know is that the shrub requires at least six weeks of cold before a branch will bloom indoors. To break dormancy, just supply warmth, sunlight and moisture.

But I learned one other interesting fact from forcing forsythia years ago. If you have a limited budget for new plants for your garden, you rapidly learn how to propagate new plants from your older ones. After my blossoms had fallen off the forced forsythia sitting in water, I saw little nubbins on the base of the branches and fully expected them to grow into roots and supply me some new shrubs. That didn't happen. The water simply got mucky with nary a root in sight. I ended up just throwing everything out and gave it no more thought.

Later that season while puttering around, I chanced on some established forsythias whose branch tips had arched over, touched the soil and promptly began rooting. The proverbial light bulb went off and now I have many forsythias all around the garden periphery. All I have to do is bend over a likely branch—one long enough to reach the soil without cracking—and simply put a heavy stone on it to anchor the tip in place. The plant does the rest. Then the following season I lift the stone, cut the newly rooted section away from the mother plant and find a good home for the baby bush.

This phenomenon is known as simple layering and while I have never tried it with any other shrubs, apparently it can also be done with climbing roses, rhododendron, boxwood and azalea.

Forsythia (*Forsythia suspensa*) are members of the *Oleaceae* family, best known for olives. Other members of the family include the common privet (*Ligustrum ovaliafolium*), Star Jasmine (*Jasmium multiflorum*) and that deliciously fragrant fall-blooming shrub *Osmanthus fragrans* as well as those perennial favorites, lilacs.

One oddity about forsythias is the belief that it produces lactose which is a sugar normally found only in mammalian milk. Recent work, however, has failed to confirm this finding.

The genus *forsythia* was named in honor of William Forsyth, a Scottish botanist (1737–1804) who relocated to London in 1763. After working at the Chelsea Physic Garden, he became its curator in 1771. In 1804, he was one of the founders of the Royal Horticultural Society.

So, when this year's forsythia flowers finally fade, I'll be out with my pruners ensuring that next spring's flowers will be the extravaganza that I have grown to expect.

Two Hundred Million Years of Ginkgo

TREES MAY NOT BE ETERNAL, but a continuous existence of 200 million years is certainly impressive. Ginkgos (*Ginkgo biloba*), which have been widely known from the fossil record, grew on all the continents at one time but gradually declined until just a few trees were left in eastern and south-central China in the 1940s. Today, it is widely grown as a street tree because it can handle difficult urban environments.

When I mentioned to a friend who lived on a street with four ginkgos along the curb, how excited I was to see a living ginkgo, he replied, "Oh, the stinky tree."

Ginkgo trees are either male or female, and the fruit obviously can only be found on female specimens. That fruit has a smell that is indeed quite awful, due to its butyric acid component, as I found out one November when I actually sniffed one. I suddenly realized that "stinky" was not an exaggeration. The smell, though, probably attracts certain animals that, after eating the pulp, deposit the seed in new locations and thereby "plant" a new crop of trees. That mechanism developed a long, long time ago but it leaves one wondering exactly what kind of animal back then found that noxious pulp attractive.

Ginkgos, both male and female, grow all over my own neighborhood. Since the gender of a ginkgo cannot be established until the tree is around thirty years old and quite tall, the current solution to the odor problem is to plant male trees exclusively. This is accomplished by simply propagating new trees from cuttings taken from mature male trees only.

Still, it's best not to pick up any large berries lying at the foot of an unidentified tree and take a whiff.

Acorns Falling All Around

YOU KNOW IT'S AUGUST when you start hearing a regular *thump, thump, thump* outdoors throughout the day. That's your oak tree (*Quercus*) flinging acorns down on your head, with the squirrels joining in the fun. They tend to stuff themselves with the best parts and throw away the less-tasty bits. One day you turn around and realize that your yard is heavily covered with acorns—large and small, whole and chewed. And if your patio does double duty as a basketball court, each game begins with a thorough sweeping.

Every summer, I plant tomatoes. Yet looking around at the abundance of acorns littering the ground, it feels terribly wasteful to take hundreds of pounds of these nuts and throw them into the recycling bin. Surely, they could be put to better use!

In fact, acorns have been used as food around the world through the centuries. Amerindians generally ate them as a foraged food; in California, it actually was a mainstay of the diet. However, acorns must be treated before eating since they are full of tannins—a chemical whose name is derived from *tanna*, the Old German word for oak trees. Tannins were used in the tanning of leather and are poisonous, so, before using acorns as food, the tannins must be thoroughly leached out using a water treatment.

Last year I discovered that there are two methods for extracting the tannins from acorns. One uses hot water, the other cold. Just for fun, and because you can never tell where the next interesting culinary marvel will come from, I decided to try preparing some acorns for eating. Since the hot water method seemed the fastest, I tried it first. It turns out that even *that* method took a fair amount of both time and water. In the middle of the process, I simply ran out of steam, so I have yet to sample my first breakfast of hot acorn mush.

And yet, watching the squirrels scarfing down the acorns, I began thinking about wildlife, which depend on garden and forest fruits that we either ignore or cannot eat. A mature oak forest can produce 700 pounds of acorns per acre, and an older tree can yield 150,000 nuts. My sixty-foot red oak (*Quercus rubra*), which is estimated to be a hundred years old, seems to be sharing almost that number of nuts with me.

As fall progresses, I expect to see the returning dark-eyed juncoes hovering over, and eating, my echinacea's seed heads. There is also heightened interest from city folk in foraging wild plants. Sadly, foraging can be a double-edged sword. When Europeans first landed in the New World, the Indians they encountered were able to live off the land in a way that most of us today cannot even imagine. However, if too many people start taking to the woods to harvest edibles, greater pressure is put upon the competing wildlife, that have nowhere else to "shop." Still, for the sheer pleasure of understanding our natural world more deeply, "Wildman" Steve Brill has been leading exciting foraging tours in our area for years. The New York Botanical Gardens also has several classes to enable us to recognize and appreciate local edibles.

Wild food is collectively known as "mast," from an old English word meaning "nuts of the forest." Parenthetically, there is even an artisanal pork product known "acorn-finished pork" in which the meat comes from pigs that forage for forest nuts.

Mast comes in two forms, hard and soft. *Hard mast* refers to the nuts of various trees such as acorns, hickory, and beechnuts. East of the Rockies, oak trees (the genus name *Quercus* means "beautiful tree") are the most important source of mast. West of the Rockies, they run second to pine trees. *Soft mast* is everything else: buds, berries, and stone fruits such as peaches. Soft mast plants include hawthorns, roses, mountain ash, and sugar maples.

And what of the wildlife species that depend on an acorn bounty? More than 150 species do, including deer, squirrels (which eat some, bury some, and generally act as oak gardeners), opossums, and bears. I've even seen a blue jay eat small pieces of acorn discarded by squirrels.

With more acorns pelting me every day, I've decided to look on YouTube again for instructions on how to make them edible. Maybe I'll go out later, collect a basketful and see what I'm missing!

Olive Harvest Recreates Ancient Agriculture

OVER THE YEARS, the Metropolitan Museum of Art has hosted several Van Gogh exhibitions and I clearly remember the magnificent fields and trees from the 1986 show *Van Gogh in Saint-Rémy and Auvers*. One particularly memorable painting was entitled *The Olive Orchard*. Van Gogh was certainly not the only artist enchanted by olive trees. Indeed, they fascinated European painters from El Greco to Monet as well as American painters including John Singer Sargent and William Merritt Chase.

Invariably, we come to Israel for the holiday of Sukkot—the Harvest Festival. The weather in Israel is generally milder than in New York at that season, and the entire country is caught up in a holiday mood.

Nothing in my New York garden really qualifies as a harvest. However, we do have the opportunity to participate in the olive harvest—a *masik*—while we are in Israel at this time. You can always tell the importance of an event when a culture has a specific word for it and it alone. The word *masik* applies exclusively to the harvesting of olives.

We return yearly to a hillside overlooking Wadi Zarka, adjacent to Neve Tzuf/Halamish in the Samarian hills, to an olive orchard planted by the Drs. Amy and Michael Rosenbluh.

In their professional lives, Michael Rosenbluh whose Ph.D. is from M.I.T., is Chairman of the Physics Department at Bar Ilan University; his specialty is light and its interaction with matter. Amy whose PhD. is from Tel Aviv University, is the Laboratory and Production director for Izun Pharma, Ltd., a research company that develops medical devices and pharmaceuticals to treat inflammatory and chronic wound conditions.

Over the years, I have watched their orchard mature from skinny saplings planted in 2000 to mature trees that now require topping. They grow two different olive species. The Barnea, developed by the Volcani Institute in Israel—a research institute for dealing with Israel's agricultural and water issues—and the Tzouri.

The Barnea was chosen because of its mild-tasting high oil yield which is appealing to Western palates. It does, unfortunately, require irrigation. The Tzouri has a larger, rounder fruit, yielding a more pungent oil but the trees do not require the additional water that can only be supplied by irrigation. This combination guarantees the

Rosenbluhs a more reliable harvest and a unique blend of oil bouquets.

Last week we visited them in order to participate once again in the *masik*. Tarpaulins were laid beneath the trees, and the lower branches were stripped of their fruit by hand. The olive fruit starts off green, ripening to an eggplant purple and finally to black. Although I had some familiarity with the process, experienced workers could "milk" an entire branch with a hard downward stroke onto the tarpaulin much more quickly than I could. Ladders are needed to reach the higher branches, whose fruit is just flung down onto the tarpaulin. When the tree is stripped of all its fruit, the olives are gathered up and poured into burlap bags for processing. The best yield to date has been 110 gallons of oil from 2,700 pounds of fruit. The oil has found a ready market as the boutique brand Tzuf Olive.

The life of an olive farmer is not easy, however. Olives are subject to several diseases and pests including the olive fruit fly (*Bactrocera oleae*), peacock spot fungus (*Spilocaea oleaginea*), and the olive moth (*Prays oleae*). Since the olives are being grown organically, methods available to control these pests are limited.

Feral pigs are also a terrible problem. They are drawn to the orchard, primarily by the irrigation water. In the process, however, they uproot new saplings, chew up young trees, and destroy the irrigation hoses.

Afterwards, we visited Tel Hazor, an enormous excavation of layered Canaanite and Israelite cities in the Galilee. We had been there years before, and I had clear memories of the extensive and impressive water system, which I wanted to revisit. That system, built by the Israelite King Ahab (died in 852 BCE), was indeed as impressive as I remembered with a 148-foot shaft dug through basalt down to underground water. Excavations had also uncovered an earlier

Canaanite ceremonial palace and layered remnants of a huge city that housed up to 15,000 people and existed for 1,000 years.

What is the relevance of Hazor to olives? Ancient olive presses are found in excavations all over Israel. In Hazor they had a particularly well-preserved press that clearly illustrated the process of producing the oil. First, olives were crushed in a basalt basin. Then they were transferred to a woven reed basket and set atop the press bed. Pressure was exerted by a beam from which stone weights were suspended. Finally the oil was collected in a jar that was partially buried for stability in the courtyard floor.

Olives were a mainstay of the ancient economy all around the Mediterranean basin. Today's groves magnificently evoke the past.

Trees Need Attention Too

D ESPITE THE OBVIOUS BENEFITS of an apartment, I had always wanted a house. In time, my husband and I had a chance to buy one.

Walking around prospective properties, you tend to check out the ambiance, the flower beds, the open space for children to play in. Sometimes the trees get overlooked.

If you're very lucky, however, there will be one or more tall specimens that will provide shade in the summer and whose mere presence provides balm to the soul. In our backyard we are lucky to have a tall red oak (*Quercus rubra*) that, in the words of our arborist, "is almost perfectly shaped." (I resent the "almost.")

Naively, we tend to think of trees caring for themselves. Trees actually require regular maintenance, mainly pruning to remove dead branches. Clearly that process is the source of the expression "getting rid of dead wood." Arborists also take the opportunity during pruning to shape the tree's growth into the most beautiful form possible. Major storms topple many trees, and squirrels tear off twigs in a form of "natural" pruning.

Bob Whitney, now a retired tree-worker, poetically described his profession. He tells the story of Michelangelo, who would begin a sculpture by examining his block of stone carefully from all sides. He felt he was not, in fact, creating a particular statue as much as liberating the form that already existed inside the block. Whitney sees the pruning of trees as a kindred process, creating a living sculpture.

Watching the young man, not surprisingly called the "climber," who ascended the tree trunks to dizzying heights in order to remove dead branches, or to begin the process of taking down a tree, is to renew your respect for those invisible workers who profoundly and positively impact our lives.

According to Whitney, tree pruning requires a combination of strategic planning, spatial configuration, and applied physics. Taking down an entire tree on the interior of a property can be time-consuming, since it must be done sequentially. First, the branches have to be removed and lowered by rope, and then the trunk is cut into segments and lowered one by one. On the other hand, when access from a street allows use of a bucket ladder, I have seen a Parks Department crew take down and completely remove a thirty-foot street tree in fifty minutes.

Rope techniques for tree work appear deceptively low-tech. The origins of our present-day methods lie with English and Irish sailors who had to devise methods to manage the raising and lowering of the various sails on long-ago sailing ships. Many sailors, upon retirement, settled in Manhattan and subsequently worked as arborists.

Walking through Riverdale, you can easily spot pruned street trees. Like scabs healing on a person's arm, there is a clear formation of healing wound tissue where a branch has been removed. These distinctive formations are referred to as "tree calluses." When the cuts are small, the calluses will eventually grow into a complete circle with a rolled edge around the cut portion. The freshly cut spot, which the callus will surround and eventually cover over, is called a "rot pocket." When branches larger than four feet in diameter are cut away, it poses a problem, since the cut will rarely heal over the rot pocket entirely, and eventually trunk decay will ensue.

Wood decay conjures up only negative images. But Nature is in constant flux, with new growth morphing into mature growth which, in turn, eventually decays in an endlessly repeating cycle. We should not be surprised, therefore, that decaying trees provide natural benefits. Dead and dying trees that remain standing are referred to by conservationists as "snags." Many birds depend on the cavities in these trees, among them nuthatches, brown creepers, and woodpeckers who forage for insects inside the tree. Mammals denning in hollow trees include squirrels, opossums, raccoons, bats, and skunks.

Nothing goes to waste in the natural world. It does, however, require patience to discern their new purposes.

I Smell Cloves

Y EARS AGO, I WAS A DOCENT at a public garden, leading Sunday afternoon tours. In order to properly prepare for my tours, I would visit the garden the preceding week, so that I could see plants that were newly blooming and be sure to showcase them.

Wandering around in early April 2016 on a back road generally ignored on tours, I was suddenly struck by a delightful, clove-like scent that I had never encountered before. There were many plants along that roadway but this was both unexpected and very special.

Systematically, I started down both sides of the road, sniffing anything with a flower. Finally, I approached a large bush, about five feet high and eight feet wide, which I had never particularly noticed before. It was pleasant enough in appearance, but there was nothing particularly memorable about it. At that moment, however, it was covered with small yellow flowers, and *bingo!*

I looked all around for the plant label and discovered that it was a *Ribes odoratum,* which I had never heard of before. It is commonly known as buffalo currant, but I have learned that it is also, aptly named, the clove currant. The scientific name derives from the Danish word *Ribs,* meaning "red currant," and *odoratus,* from the Latin meaning "fragrant." Sometimes disagreement occurs over exact scientific nomenclature, and this plant is also listed as *Ribes aureum* var. *villosum.* It is native to the central United States, specifically from Minnesota to South Dakota, and south all the way to Arkansas and Texas.

In order to achieve fruiting, both a male and female plant are required. Unfortunately, there is a downside to this *Ribes.* It can act as a host to pine blister rust—*Cronartium ribicola*—which is fatal to white pines (*Pinus strobus*), and apparently at one time there were serious restrictions on the planting of *Ribes odoratum* in the Northeast. However, a cultivar named Crandall is available which is very resistant or even immune to blister rust.

Fragrance adds charm to any garden. As I walk through unfamiliar gardens, I am always checking flowers for scent. The hyacinths are blooming now in my garden, to be followed by lily-of-the-valley, lilacs and peonies, and finally roses.

Herb growers know, many plants also have scented leaves. To enjoy those scents, all that is required is a light rubbing of the leaves between the fingers, and the fragrance is briefly transferred to the fingertips for sniffing. One of my favorite plants for leaf rubbing is the wild type 'geranium' called "cranesbill" based on the shape of the seed pod which blooms in early spring and whose leaves smell of citronella. There are additional plants (*Perlargoniums*) specifically cultivated for scents such as lemon, cinnamon, nutmeg, and roses.

To confuse matters further, *Perlargoniums* are also commonly referred to as geraniums. While they are related plants and are both members of the botanical family *Geraniaceae*, they belong to two different genera.

I visited the New York Botanical Garden's annual orchid show, aptly named that year, Orchidelirium. As I opened the doors leading into the exhibition hall, I was overwhelmed by the strength of the flower perfume.

As if that were not pleasure enough, the gardenias (*Gardenia jasminoides*) were blooming in an adjacent Conservatory room. I completely fell in love with their fragrance when a friend sent us a single flower with instructions to float it in a bowl of water. One such flower was enough to perfume the entire room.

So to return full circle to our *Ribes odoratum*: Whenever I would take a tour through that garden during those critical weeks in early April, I would always take the group down that back lane and asked them to sniff and locate the responsible plant. Everyone always found the right bush!

Insects

A Butterfly Lover's Delight

I AM WILLING TO BET THAT YOU TOO love butterflies! I suspect most people do, although few have much interest in, or affinity for, insects generally.

Years ago, we were privileged to visit the Monarch Butterfly Sanctuary in Pacific Grove (CA) where we saw huge clusters of butterflies hanging from eucalyptus and pine trees. They were huddled together in pendulous bundles and were so nondescript that, at first, we didn't even realize that we were seeing the actual overwintering monarchs. Apparently, they form these long clusters, resembling nothing more exciting than dead leaves, to conserve heat. The trees offer a perfect microclimate, providing the necessary humidity, light, shade, temperature, and protection from the wind. The eucalyptus trees also provide the nectar nourishment that the butterflies require when the temperature warms above 55°F., allowing them to fly and feed.

But there are so many other butterflies that are just as beautiful. When we travel, if we see a butterfly house listed as a tourist attraction, we visit it. Most exhibits have few butterflies relative to the volume of the butterfly houses, though, and it's practically impossible to see them clearly, let alone photograph them.

Locally, however, we are very fortunate to have the Butterfly Garden exhibit at the Bronx Zoo available to us every summer. The original exhibit opened in 1996. The open area where the multitudes of butterflies and moths—both of which are members of the order *Lepi-*

doptera—swoop freely is under a netting with double doors at each end to prevent escapees.

Meandering through the netted area, is a path lined with feeding stations, flowering plants, and trees. You feel as if you are in a primeval garden, watching butterflies alight wherever they can freely sip on nectar. Sometimes they even land on a person's shoulder or head, making for a great photo op. Sometimes, they seem to be sunning themselves or snoozing, perching for long minutes in one spot, wings wide open. This gives photographers time to focus for a great close-up. Other times, a butterfly will remain stationary for several minutes while slowly opening and closing its wings—a much more challenging shot. I have even seen some perched on the netting overhead as if they were posing. With a zoom lens, you can get terrific pictures.

The butterfly exhibit also includes an incubator in which caterpillars complete successful molts, first to the pupal stage and finally to the dramatically colored adult. Most of the pupae are brownish and unremarkable, but some are an attractive aquamarine.

To round off the butterfly imagery, there is a pool filled with butterfly koi. If you have never seen these magnificent fish, let me describe them. We have all seen goldfish, both large and small. They are a form of carp, originally bred over a thousand-year period in China for various colors—orange, white, yellow, and red-white mixes.

Koi were developed in Japan in the 1820s. To my eye, they look like oversized goldfish. But *butterfly* koi. . .they are indeed something special. Developed in the mid-twentieth century by Japanese breeders seeking greater hardiness in the standard koi, their fins and tails are greatly enlarged, and the fish appear to be trailing long, graceful diaphanous scarves as they swim.

Today, home gardeners share many ecological concerns. Interest in native plants is high, and many gardeners want to attract butterflies to their gardens. Necessary factors for doing so include food—various nectar-producing plants that bloom in succession over the summer, water, wind-breaking shrubs or tall plants, as well as rocks to bask on. There are so many plants, both perennial and annual, that attract specific butterflies. For example, clover attracts sulphurs and whites, parsley attracts black and anise swallowtails, violets attract fritillaries, and hollyhocks attract painted ladies. The opportunities are endless.

For years, I have seen a red admiral perch on exactly the same location next to my front door. Since butterflies do not survive from one year to the next, I can only wonder what is attracting successive generations to that spot. We see swallowtails of all varieties throughout the summer. I am already on the lookout!

Recycling Experiment

A LONG TIME AGO, WHILE IN COLLEGE, I worked part-time in a genetics lab. The organism of choice for these experiments was the lowly *Drosophila melanogaster*—our common fruit fly. They are excellent subjects because their genetics are simpler than mammals', they are small and easily handled, and large populations could be kept in small bottles. Since their entire life-cycle could be completed in two weeks, it is possible to follow induced mutations over several generations. Today, fruit flies are simply a minor kitchen nuisance brought into the house on summer fruit or bananas.

Our home recently (2016) received a brown can from the New York City Department of Sanitation strictly for organic recycling, and I have been dutifully placing all my organic kitchen waste in it. While approving wholeheartedly of the recycling concept, I had not enjoyed the smelly mess that remained after garbage pickup, or the necessary cleanup, since plastic can liners were initially prohibited. (It is now legal to use them).

Several weeks ago, I was outside preparing to clean out the recycling can when I suddenly paid attention to the fact that there were many small, brown cocoons attached to the lid of the can, as well as numerous insect larvae crawling around inside. Because of my background with *Drosophila*, I thought it would be interesting to hatch out the insects and isolate the adult flies, which I assumed, would be my old friends the fruit flies.

I placed some vegetable peelings into a glass jar, made air holes in the lid, lifted twenty larvae out of the can, and put them into the jar. I examined the jar daily, and about twelve days later I had a whole group of flies crawling up the inside of the jar. They were small and looked similar to fruit flies, but I always like to consult with an expert before stating something categorically. I consulted an entomologist friend but it was not his area of expertise. He did, however, voice some skepticism about my conclusion, saying that he could not confidently identify them as *Drosophila*. I then remembered fruit flies have red eyes, and my specimens didn't.

I turned next to the New York City Department of Sanitation, assuming they must have entomologists on staff who would be familiar, not only with such questions, but with pests that are commonly found in garbage. They were very accessible but demurred on an identification without a photo.

In the lab, we used ether to anesthetize our flies; I had no such material handy nowadays. They gave me several good suggestions about how to isolate and immobilize a fly so as to photograph it properly. With a decent photograph in hand, I finally received an answer.

Indeed, they were not fruit flies but phorid flies—otherwise known as "humpbacked flies."

Although the number is probably not exhaustive, there seem to be four types of small flies that one might encounter around the home. Fruit flies and phorid flies have already been mentioned. In addition, there are drain flies and sphaerocerid flies. While all of these are members of the scientific order *Diptera*, they each belong to different families. *Drosophila* are *Drosophilidae*, the phorid flies are *Phoridae*, the drain flies (which look moth-like and are, therefore, called "moth flies") are in the family *Psychodidae*, and the sphaerocerid flies are members of the *Sphaeroceridae* family. Their other commonality is that they are all found in damp areas with rotting vegetation, garbage, or sewage.

The burning question for homeowners is how to get rid of them. Careful cleaning is always the first step. After that, the internet is full of solutions, some of which I have found useful. Fruit flies have also been called "vinegar flies," since they cannot resist cider vinegar. A common suggestion for ridding your kitchen of fruit flies involves securely covering a partially filled bottle of cider vinegar with plastic wrap. Poke a small hole in the plastic. The flies enter and cannot leave.

Hatching your own flies might not be as intriguing as hatching butterflies, but it makes a good experiment to do with children.

Lubber Grasshoppers

DURING CHILDHOOD, SUMMER DAYS stretch out in endless, glorious hours, and one of our favorite activities was to catch grasshoppers. While most insects did not make the cut, certain ones seemed cute and could be incorporated into play.

To catch a grasshopper, you just needed a good eye and quick re-flexes. You had to track their trajectory, get to their landing area fast, and cup your hands over them before they took off again. The joy was solely in the effort. You immediately released them and then did it all over again.

On a spring driving trip South, our final destination was the Ever-glades, that mythical swamp that stretches over large swaths of south-ern Florida. The best part about traveling in May is that the weather is warm and there are no crowds.

There are three types of terrain in the Everglades—mangrove swamps, grasslands, and bald cypress swamps. We joined a swamp buggy tour, essentially a bus on huge tires, that took us through grass-lands and bald cypress swamps. I had no trouble securing a seat by an open window. While the swamp apparently teems with assorted wildlife, all we saw were white-tailed deer, including some adorable fawns, and a manatee that was so busy cooling off in a channel that all we saw was the top of its head. However, as I was hanging through the open window, I saw a multitude of highly colored small 'somethings' in motion all along our grassy path. When I inquired about them, what I thought I heard through the roar of the engine was "lover grasshopper," which sounded improbable. It turned out that this insect, richly jeweled in tones of yellow, orange, and black, was the Eastern lubber grasshopper—*Romalea microptera*.

As usual when discussing the natural world, nothing is straight-forward, and a few terms need to be considered. I have always used "grasshopper' and "cricket" as interchangeable terms. That's not cor-rect. "Locust" and "grasshopper" are more correctly interchangeable terms. However, grasshoppers are generally solitary insects, while locusts are particular grasshopper species gone wild. Those benign grasshoppers who can convert to destructive locusts undergo this behavioral change when population explosions lead to excessive crowding. Under those conditions, when one grasshopper touches the hind wing of another, it causes an increase in serotonin production in the brain. This hormone changes normal grasshoppers into swarming locusts, which go on eating frenzies that can devastate entire countries, leading to severe famines. Fortunately only about ten of the eight thousand grasshopper species can swarm.

Finally, there is an insect called a "katydid" that gets lumped in with the others.

All of these insects belong to the order *Orthoptera*, meaning "straight wings" (from the Greek *ortho*—"straight or rigid," referring to the front wing—and *ptera*, "winged.") The sub-order *Caelifera* includes the grasshoppers (which have short antennae), and the sub-order *Ensifera* contains the crickets and katydids (having antennae minimally the length of the insect's body).

Other characteristics distinguishing grasshoppers from crickets are that crickets come out at dusk while grasshoppers are active during the day. Also, grasshoppers eat grass while crickets will eat animal matter. To distinguish a katydid from a grasshopper, note that the body of the katydid is rounder and closely resembles a leaf, even having leaf-like veins on the body. They likewise eat animal matter. There are numerous other structural differences among these species, but most of us will not hold an insect in our hands long enough to inspect it that closely.

The Eastern lubber grasshopper's range is North Carolina to Florida and westward to Texas. They can be found in open pine woods, weedy fields, and roadside vegetation, which explains my sighting. They lay their eggs in the ground after summer mating. The eggs then overwinter and hatch in the spring warmth. Grasshoppers develop into adults through a process called incomplete metamorphosis. This means that, although the juvenile, which looks like a miniature adult, will molt and shed its thin exoskeleton as it grows, it never forms a cocoon from which a physically different adult will emerge. They undergo a total of five molts at fifteen-day intervals. Unfortunately, the lubbers prefer to eat the foliage of citrus trees, vegetables, and ornamental plants.

While the lubbers do not swarm, they are a problem in agricultural areas. Control methods include clearing away woody debris, turning over the soil where they lay eggs, the use of pesticides as the eggs hatch, and the use of a fungus—*Metarhzium*—also used on locusts.

All that glitters is not gold!

Queen of the Garden

I SPEND A LOT OF TIME AT MY COMPUTER, and, one August, I sensed motion on the plants immediately outside my window. The Joe-Pye weed (genus *Eutrochium*)was blooming well that year, and atop the long stalks I saw a gorgeous Monarch butterfly (*Danaus plexippus*) alighting on the mound of small pink flowers. I let out a yell, and everyone in the house came running.

By now, the public is well aware that the Monarch is endangered. The number of butterflies returning to their overwintering sites in California and Mexico has shrunk, as demonstrated by the reduced amount of acreage covered by butterflies at these sanctuaries.

Two years ago, I planted a milkweed plant (*Asclepias syriaca*) in my effort to induce them to visit my garden. Despite assuming that having the word "weed" in the plant name would mean that I might have way too many plants within a few years, I never saw mine again. So, last year I went out and bought another milkweed that had finished blooming but was filled with seed pods in the hope that either the mother plant or the seeds would provide me with many more Monarch opportunities.

According to the United States Department of Agriculture (USDA), seeds should be collected from the ripe pods before they split open. The seeds, which have silky sails, are dispersed by the wind, and once the pod opens, the seeds will quickly disappear. Since they require chilling for three months for successful germination, they should be planted in the fall if you try collecting and sowing your seeds. Otherwise they can be chilled in the refrigerator over the winter and sown while the soil is still quite cool in the spring.

Our view of Monarchs is far too simplistic. The general story line is they overwinter far away, migrate across the U.S. during the spring, and return to their winter sites in the fall. But so much more is happening beneath the radar!

In fact, the spring-migrating butterflies are long dead by the following fall, and it is their great-great-grandchildren who are "returning" to places they have never seen. Those great-great-grandparents lived four to five months in their winter location, supposedly in the same trees that their ancestors hibernated on—eucalyptus trees in California, oyamel fir trees in Mexico.

In February–March the butterflies begin to awaken, mate, and start their northward migration. (Incidentally, according to migration maps, our New York Monarchs are actually coming from either Mexico or southern Florida.) March–April sees the first generation, May–

June the second, July–August the third, and September–October the fourth. This final generation migrates southward for the winter and does not mate until February–March, when it begins the northward migration and the cycle continues.

Monarch females need to lay their eggs on one of several different varieties of milkweed plants. The female will not lay more than one egg per plant, since the caterpillar is a voracious eater and proper spacing of the young better guarantees sufficient food. The egg is attached on the underside of a leaf and hatches four days later into a caterpillar. The caterpillar is an eating machine, and as it grows too fat for its skin, it molts—sheds the old skin—five times over 10 to 14 days, growing from 2–6mm all the way to 25–45mm in length. It then forms a cocoon, and the pupa inside metamorphoses over 10 to 14 days, emerging as the black, gold, and orange creature that we so look forward to. The adults, with the exception of the migrating generation, live only 2–5 weeks

Upon reaching its adult form, Monarchs stop eating milkweed leaves and, instead, require nectar-producing plants to feed on. Spring-flowering nectar plants include chives, Siberian wallflower, and May night sage (*Salvia sylvestris*). Flowers that bloom later in the season, picking up when the milkweed leaves off, include blue cardinal flower, zinnias, and our Joe-Pye weed. It should be noted that alkaloids derived from their milkweed diet make both Monarch caterpillars and adults unpalatable and even poisonous to predators.

But are lack of habitat and milkweed shortage the only problems that Monarchs face? Hardly! Three other factors are now being cited as well. One is called "habitat fragmentation." Highways now crisscross our country, and many butterflies end up smashing into cars as they migrate. Factor two is bad weather, and three is loss of the nectar producing plants that the adults need. Drought, floods, and other severe weather conditions impact heavily on the availability of nectar-producing flowers that the butterflies need in order to migrate safely and maintain health.

Seemingly straightforward problems frequently mask a myriad of other important factors, each of which requires careful consideration.

Birds

Birds in a Snowstorm

OUR GOOD FRIEND RABBI CHARLES SHEER has been our resident birdwatcher and go-to person for anything pertaining to little feathered creatures. My personal interest in the natural world was once limited to botany, geology, and evolution, and while I was always impressed by the sheer color and variety of the birds whenever we visited the Bronx Zoo, I really could not work up any further enthusiasm for them.

But, one winter morning, I poured birdseed into a bowl, hung a suet block (fat mixed with birdseed, which delivers high- energy food) from the top of the birdfeeder, and waited to see what kinds of birds would show up. I saw all the familiar players—robins, jays, cardinals, juncos, and sparrows. Since I had never seen any other varieties, I didn't think free seed would bring out any unfamiliar species. I was so wrong! So far I have seen three different types of woodpeckers, cowbirds, doves, grackles, starlings, mockingbirds, and titmice.

The first snowstorm of 2016 left a heavy accumulation of snow in Riverdale. I had put out seed the night before and covered it with a plastic bag to protect it during the night. I had also made sure that there was a fresh block of suet hanging there. In the morning, I removed the plastic covering from the food dish and assumed that there would be minimal activity at the feeder since, surely, the birds would stay huddled wherever they go for protection at night and wait out the storm. Was I in for a surprise!

Practically every species of bird that I had ever seen made an appearance that day, at times mobbing the feeder. Species that rarely showed interest in the suet block were regularly alighting on the cage and pecking at the block between the metal strands of the holder. And as snow started to accumulate on top of the seed bowl, some of the birds used their wings to flap it out.

According to the *New York Times*, about a fifth of all Americans feed birds. Watching birds on a normal day is entrancing enough, but realizing that I now had responsibilities to my local birds has spurred me to see that that feeder is carefully tended daily.

Birdfeeder Bully

AS A NEWBIE TO BIRD FEEDING AND BIRDFEEDERS, I have gotten a lot of advice. I have heard that blue jays are the bullies of the backyard. They squawk loudly and push their weight around. I have always thought that they are particularly beautiful birds with their gorgeous plumage, though, so I was wondering how I would feel about them as time went on.

When you first start putting out seed in a feeder, you wait anxiously for days for anything to show up. When they finally arrive you wonder, "How do they know that food is available right here?", a question I still cannot answer.

As time went on, birds of different species continued to arrive. After about five months of this, I can honestly say that I regularly have representatives of ten genera—with a total of fourteen different species—showing up. And these are just those birds that don't migrate with the coming of the cold weather. I can't wait to see how many more will show up when warm weather arrives.

Anyway, my focus today is literally on the "pecking order." Personally, I must say that blue jays get a bad rap. Yes, they are large, and yes they are noisy, but I do not find them particularly belligerent. The prize for belligerency actually goes to the mourning dove!

When my first dove showed up at the feeder, I was quite excited. I had seen them occasionally, and we have such rosy expectations of doves given the iconic symbolism of the "dove of peace."

But: To begin with, the dove is a large bird, and size is always a factor in animal behavior. The general feeding pattern is for birds of all sizes to show up, grab a few seeds, fly away, and return again later. The dove, however, is not in a hurry. It lands by the food bowl and eyes it. If another bird shows up, including other doves, it carefully shoos it away, pecking seed leisurely over the rim. After feeding uninterrupted for several minutes, it still does not leave. It clambers over the edge of the bowl and settles into it as if it were nesting there, protecting it from any other bird foolish enough to expect food.

Apparently, the large amount of seed that the dove does eat at one sitting is not going directly into the stomach. Instead it is stored in the bird's crop—an expanded pouch anterior to the stomach—for later digestion. Perhaps I'll make a point one day of checking to see how long a dove will sit guarding its treasure.

Every morning, I put out a cup of mixed seeds, and that amount serves a large number of birds—the doves and their competitors—for hours. Expert advice, meanwhile, tells me that if I put out only large, striped sunflower seeds and peanuts still in the shell, the doves won't show up: Their beaks are too narrow to swallow the seeds with the shells intact and not strong enough to break and extract the meat. (Addendum: I tried the sunflower seeds and the doves were not deterred).

But how does the dove's belligerence square with its symbolic association? That symbolism stems from the story of Noah and the Flood, in which the dove returns to Noah with an olive sprig in its beak, demonstrating that the Flood is over and that the earth was blooming again. Most likely Noah sent the dove out to scout the land because of its strength and perseverance. A weaker bird might not have been able to return with the olive branch in its beak. Seemingly, it is the olive branch alone that is the symbol of peace. It grows under adverse conditions, providing essential food to those willing to work for it—and the dove is tough enough to bring the news.

If the doves weren't so troublesome, I would more happily entertain their presence.

Riverdale's Hummingbirds

I FINALLY SAW MY FIRST HUMMINGBIRD this season (2016), and it wasn't even at my hummingbird feeder, which I had so carefully tended; instead, it was fluttering around a flowering red bee balm plant (*Monarda didyma*). Despite heavy traffic to my birdfeeder, I had never seen a hummingbird in my yard.

The first time I saw what I thought *might* be a hummingbird, I was a pre-teen. Something quite small was fluttering madly on the ground, seemingly entangled in long grass stalks. Having never seen anything like it before, I approached it cautiously. If it was a large—*very* large—insect, I didn't want any part of it. But if it was a hummingbird, I definitely wanted to examine it up close and certainly wanted to free it. Despite my trepidation, I tried to disentangle it but it was probably injured and couldn't seem to free itself, even with my help. I never entirely resolved the question of what I was looking at, but I now strongly suspect it was, indeed, a hummingbird.

Over the years, I have caught glimpses of them, particularly in lavishly flowered gardens. Because of their energetic flight, it has been impossible to see one clearly.

When we were in Israel in the fall of 2016, I saw a whole group of darting iridescent birds through the window and started dragging people outside to see them. While exciting in their own right, it turned out that they were an entirely different bird called a Palestine sunbird or a northern orange-tufted sunbird (*Cinnyris osea*, family *Nectariini-idae*), while our local bird is a ruby-throated hummingbird (*Archilochus colubris*, family *Trochildae*) .

In 2015 I finally went out and bought a hummingbird feeder, which is essentially an upside-down plastic bottle connected to little feeding spouts from which the birds can sip a sugar syrup you cook up in your kitchen by dissolving one part sugar in four parts water. I placed the feeder outside a kitchen window but never once saw a hummingbird go near it.

This spring I called Wild Birds Unlimited in New Jersey (201-599-0099) for advice. First they asked if the feeder was red, since this color is highly attractive to hummingbirds. Then they explained that I needed to change the syrup solution every three days. I hadn't been doing that, because I mistakenly thought that, if the bottle still contained some solution, everything was fine. Now I make up a fresh solution every week, which I refrigerate until it is time for a fresh bottle.

Still no hummingbirds. I moved the feeder into a sunnier spot. That didn't work either. And now I have one visiting my bee balm, found in an entirely different garden area!

Hummingbirds are among the world's tiniest birds. Their name derives from the whirring sound their wings make as they hover, lapping up nectar. Amazingly, they are capable of flying forward, backward, or sideways. Their wings beat fifty times a second, and their hearts beat 1,200 times a minute. They have the highest metabolic rate of any warm-blooded animal. At night though or when the temperature drops they go into a state of torpor (reduced metabolic activity) to reduce their caloric needs to one-fifteenth of the usual rate. This process also occurs in some marsupial species, as well as in mice and bats.

Despite the birds' prodigious physiological attributes, their feet are relatively weak. They can perch, but cannot use their feet for walking or hopping.

Bees are our most familiar pollinators, but birds are active pollinators as well. Pollination by birds is called "ornithophily." Hummingbirds, sunbirds, spiderhunters, honeycreepers, and honeyeaters are the most common bird pollinators. The plants they pollinate usually have funnel-shaped flower cups colored orange, scarlet, red, or white, and provide a strong perch. The flowers that they pollinate include shrimp plants, verbenas, bee balm (well, that makes sense), honeysuckles, fuchsias, hibiscus, and bromeliads.

As I sit here typing, I have a pot of sugar syrup on the stove. When it cools, I'll go out, wash out the feeder bottle and try to tempt my local hummingbirds with a new offering.

Our State Bird

CANADA, UNLIKE MANY OTHER COUNTRIES, did not have a national bird. Therefore, the Royal Canadian Geographic Society launched a contest asking Canadians to choose their favorite bird.

As in the U.S., where the majority does not always get its choice for president, the third-place candidate was voted in as the winner (2016). The winning bird turned out to be the gray jay, a corvid relative of ravens and our own blue jays, which came in behind the first place common loon and the second place snowy owl.

The choice—also called the whiskey jack, from the Cree Indian name *Wisakedjak*, has not sat well with voters, who are not especially familiar with this bird. While the gray jay can be found in every Canadian province, it tends to live in the northern, colder parts of those provinces, far from major population centers. The Geographic Society, however, felt it represented Canadians particularly well since the bird is friendly, very smart, hardy, and remains in Canada year round.

The choice of an unfamiliar bird for a Canadian symbol got me thinking about our own local symbols. I had absolutely no idea what the New York State bird might be. I also checked to see if New York City has a symbolic bird, which it does not. I shudder to think that it could be the pigeon! In truth, the New York State bird, which we share with Missouri, turns out to be the eastern bluebird (*Sialia sialis*), adopted officially in 1970.

To avoid the sin of omission, here's a list of the almost endless number of New York State symbols. The state tree is the sugar maple, the state shell is the bay scallop, the state fossil is the sea scorpion—*Eurypterus remipes*, from the Silurian Age (444–416 MYA), the state gem is the garnet, the state insect is the nine-spotted ladybug, the state reptile is the snapping turtle, the state animal is the beaver, the state fruit is the apple, the state flower is the rose, the state bush is the lilac, the state freshwater fish is the brook trout, and finally, the state salt water fish is the striped bass. I'm exhausted.

Why are there so many symbols? While these designations can only be created by the State Legislature, the categories are usually driven by public interest. A suitable subject is selected by individuals, students, or organizations. That symbol is then researched for appropriateness, and a request for a legislative bill is created. The bill follows a designated legislative process and, if approved, *voilà*, we have a new state symbol.

So far, I have never had an Eastern bluebird visit my birdfeeder. In fact, I've never seen one anywhere. A little research shows that only dried mealworms will entice them to a feeder since they primarily eat insects in summer. In winter, however, in the absence of insects, they will eat fruit or berries still clinging to tree branches.

The male's wings, back, and head are covered with bright blue feathers, the chest is rusty red, and the belly is white. The female has the same color scheme although her colors are more muted. The bird is a member of the thrush family (*Turdidae*) and, although small, is very fierce in defending its nest—which can be found either in a tree or a manmade nest box—from much larger birds.

In the spirit of neighborliness, I looked up the state birds for New York's two closest neighbors, New Jersey and Connecticut. New Jersey's is the Eastern or American goldfinch (*Spinus tristis*), and Connecticut's is the robin (*Turdus migratorius*). Robins are the largest North American member of the thrushes, which means it is related to the Eastern bluebird. Although I think of robins as harbingers of spring, apparently some do not migrate.

American goldfinches are just that, with the emphasis on "gold." The male's spring plumage is a brilliant yellow on the body while the wings are black and white and it wears a black cap. Male winter plumage is duller.

It might be fun to consider a symbolic Riverdale bird. With so many different ones visiting local feeders, it would be interesting to see the favorites. I'm rather partial to the black-capped chickadee, or nuthatches, or. . . .

Turkeys Galore

ON A SATURDAY AFTERNOON LAST FALL, we were having a quiet lunch when we noticed a large shape moving around the backyard. Usually, if I see a turkey, it's on my plate; but I was pretty certain I was seeing a real live one. That evening I checked Google images and, just as I thought, it was a female turkey, which has less flamboyant coloring than the male. But, having seen the occasional hawk flit through my line of sight, I assumed it was a similarly casual occurrence, not likely to be repeated.

My husband , listening to a radio news station as he drove to work, caught the tail end of a story—pardon the pun—about flocks of turkeys, as well as individual birds, seen all around Northern New Jersey. The sudden coincidence seemed too good to miss.

Since I was in Teaneck, New Jersey, later that week, I slowly drove through several neighborhoods trying to spot birds I could photograph. If I'd been tracking geese, I would have looked for wide-open lawns or parks. So I checked several of those and, in addition, drove up and down quiet residential streets. No luck. But *Green Scene* articles always include a photo. However, since I belong to a Teaneck Yahoo group, I put out a query for turkey pictures and, in a few hours, was inundated with photos—confirming the existence of large numbers of turkeys in the neighborhood.

Just this week, I was discussing the whooping crane (*Grus amer-*

icana) and the remarkable story of its resurrection as a viable species after coming close to extinction. In 1941, there were only fifteen left. Conservationists stepped in; by 1971 there were fifty-seven, and 214 were counted in 2005. Although the whooping crane is a migratory bird flying between Texas and Canada, a colony of young birds established in Florida apparently had never learned how to migrate. They had to be taught by an International Whooping Crane Recovery Team using an ultra-light aircraft. You may have seen a similar project in the movie *Fly Away Home,* where a real-life Bill Lishman and his daughter taught orphan geese how to fly south. In 2009, seventy-seven cranes followed such a plane from Florida to Wisconsin and back.

The story of the whooping cranes is relevant to our turkey tale because turkeys (*Meleagris gallopavo*) disappeared from New Jersey in the mid-1850s. In 1977, however, the New Jersey Division of Fish and Wildlife introduced twenty-two birds; their numbers have grown to over 20,000 today.

In any case, there are now enough turkeys to create problems. One memorable 911 call from the head of the Hillsdale, New Jersey, Post Office declared that a mailman had been surrounded by a flock that was acting aggressively. In another incident, a turkey crashed through the window of a private home. *That* may have happened as a result of a male turkey mistaking his reflection in the glass for another male. Since the event occurred during mating season, with its normal increase in testosterone and consequent aggression, the male turkey may have thought that he was attacking an interloper. If confronted by an aggressive turkey, it is important to know that they act within an established pecking order. It is, therefore, important not to appear afraid of them and to create dominance. The recommended methods according to the Humane Society of New Jersey include making noise, waving your arms, spraying them with a hose, popping open an umbrella, or throwing tennis balls.

Turkeys forage by scratching through leaves. Their most important food is acorns, but in winter they will eat grass seed, wild grapes, dogwood fruits, and grains. Young turkeys mainly eat insects, which provide them with needed protein.

It was thrilling to have a turkey visit our backyard that day, but given the potential problems, I am pleased that they have forgotten our address.

The Year of the Rooster

AN OVERHEARD SNIPPET OF CONVERSATION can lead to terminal curiosity. That happened to me one day when I tuned in mid-program to National Public Radio and heard an author discussing his book—about chickens, no less—and explaining how the worldwide spread of chickens was enormously important both to human culture and nutrition.

I recently bought the book, *Why Did the Chicken Cross the World?* by Andrew Lawler, and when a recent newspaper article noted that the new Chinese New Year (2017) was the Year of the Rooster, everything started falling into place.

Westerners use a solar calendar, which marks the exact time it takes the sun to return to the identical position in the sky as the Earth completes one full revolution around the sun. We tend to say that a solar year is 365 days long. However, in reality, it is 365 days, 5 hours, 49 minutes, and approximately 46 seconds long. Since a partial day is involved, we have regular leap years, with an added day included in February to compensate for that discrepancy.

Lunar calendars also exist, in which months are counted by observing a new moon, which occurs every 29.5 days. The lunar calendar has only 354.4 days in a year, which leaves an eleven-day discrepancy between it and the solar calendar. This calendar is used without any correction in the Muslim world, which is why significant events such as Ramadan cannot be pegged to a specific season.

There is also a *combination* calendar called "luni-solar," designed so that the lunar calendar inserts leap-months as needed, to provide synchrony with the solar calendar. This is done purposely so that certain holidays will occur in the proper season. It was pointed out to me years ago, for example, that Chinese New Year always falls on or close to the Jewish New Moon (Month) in February. Friday night, January 27, 2017, for example, marking the beginning of Chinese New Year (Year of the Rooster), coincided with the start of the Jewish month of Shevat.

The Chinese luni-solar calendar is quite old, with attribution going back to Huang-ti, or the Yellow Emperor, in 2,697 BCE. While the Chinese calendar uses a sixty-year cycle, the Jewish calendar, which was developed much more recently, only uses a nineteen-year cycle with extra intercalary months inserted to assure that Passover, the spring festival, actually falls in springtime.

Horoscopes and astrological readings seem to fascinate many people although I am not among them. However, many years ago, we were at a park in Hawaii that included statues of the various animals associated with each Chinese year. Twelve animals are used in a strict rotation. A plaque accompanied each statue, listing the personality characteristics of those persons born in each named year. I was amused to see that some of the associations were closer than I would have thought. *Roosters*, those born during the Year of the Rooster, are thought to be healthy and athletic, attractive and socially adept, amusing and hardworking.

The year 2017 was also the year of the Fire Rooster. Because a sixty-year cycle is running, there are other symbols that help differentiate one same-named year from another. Since there are four other elements besides fire that can fall on rooster years, I assume there must be subtle differences among these various roosters. Before 2017, the last Year of the Fire Rooster fell in 1957; other generic Years of the Rooster fell in 1969, 1981, 1993, and 2005.

Meanwhile, let us return to our fowl, the domesticated chicken (*Gallus gallus domesticus*). Years ago we were at a zoo overseas and several roosters strutted by. There are many breeds of chickens, some more colorful than others, but these roosters were exquisite, with feathers in hues of bronze, green, black, and yellow. All I could think of was, "If we weren't so busy eating them, we might really appreciate them."

The ancestor of today's chicken seems to be the red jungle fowl of South Asia, which appeared 7,000-10,000 years ago, although many of *today's* local chickens have origins on the Indian subcontinent. Archeological evidence shows them spreading west through Asia and Europe and eastward through the Pacific islands. They had multiple uses. They have served as sacrifices, oracles, and were the central element of cockfighting as well as providing a source of meat and egg protein. Until World War II, chicken was not particularly popular as a meat source in the United States, but with beef and pork needed to feed our servicemen overseas, chicken took on greater importance. In 1951 the Chicken of Tomorrow contest led to the breeding of our modern meatier varieties.

Chicken has become important enough that there are numerous terms to describe them. A male chicken is called a "rooster" in the U.S. while in the UK and Ireland, it is known as a "cock," though before it reaches its first birthday, it is called a "cockerel." Castrated males are "capons." Young female birds are called "pullets" until their first birthday or until they begin laying eggs, at which time they become "hens." Chickens raised for meat are called "broilers" and those raised for eggs are "laying hens."

Some varieties of hens can lay an egg almost every day, although they cannot keep that up for their entire lifespan. Hens will lay eggs even if they are not fertilized; however, those eggs are sterile.

One family in North Riverdale has been a regular stop for local children because of the ducks they keep in their yard. But so far, I've never seen a chicken the neighborhood!

Animals

Animals in Uganda—Up Close and Personal

(The author of the following piece, Zecharya Blau, spent three months in Uganda on Project Ten (play on words since "ten" in Hebrew means "giving"), a Peace Corps–type program run by the Israeli government. These are some of his impressions.

Antelopes gallop across the savannah, chased by roaring cheetahs. A lion tosses his mane as a zebra flees, elephants bathe in virgin rivers and silverbacks make the earth shudder with each knuckle-swinging step. The camera tilts up a giraffe's neck, through the leafy canopy he's decimating, and catches a crested crane wheeling around.

The above paragraph is what I expected to find in Uganda. I arrived driven and motivated to make the most of my three months of volunteering, but also excited and ready to be awed and dazzled by parts of the animal kingdom I'd only seen on a screen. Dogs and cats are boringly domesticated, while livestock is boring period. Even the occasional jackal nearby my home whose howls kept me up at night had become passé. I wanted something new, different, pictures to show, stories to impress with. The third day after landing one of my colleagues saw a monkey, and we were all green with envy.

In the end we did see those sights. The flora and fauna in Man's first continent is rich and diverse, and it's certainly not what we were used to seeing in our urban locales. Monkeys with electric blue testicles jumped up and down on our aluminum roofing, causing widespread insomnia and boosting Uganda's leading sleeping pill company's revenue through two quarters. Said monkeys also attacked members of the group on some occasions, luckily without inflicting any physical harm. Crested cranes were everywhere, proving that their position as the national bird is apt, and so were antelopes. Zebras were spotted from afar on a boat trip, though a small argument whether they weren't perhaps only "speckled horses" ensued and was only settled by the use of our guide's binoculars. Several of my friends went on safaris and were lucky enough to see elephants, hippopotami, giraffes, myriad big cats and innumerable avian species. No one had the money to spend on gorilla tracking, but one of our compound's guards had worked in Bwindi Impenetrable National Park and he assured us that the legendary silverbacks actually, truly exist. It was all thrilling.

As we got down to our actual volunteering, following the orientation week, I was immediately thrown off the deep end. Armed only with some chalk and a beat-up textbook, I stood in front of forty blankly staring faces whose grasp of English was surprisingly good but of an American accent astoundingly weak, trying to explain verb tenses. The second grade classroom was roofless and separated from third grade by a wall that was no more than spaced wooden planks, letting every sound and murmur from the older children sidle in. Students shared pencils and an eraser. An eraser, singular. The smell of feces from the latrines dominated our mornings, while afternoons were the domain of odors from the fishmongers' stalls. As though this wasn't enough, animals constantly invaded our domicile of learning, small yet loudly-buzzing gnats, plagues of grasshoppers, the occasional pet and more often real, flesh-and-blood livestock—your common cow or goat, strolling by our educational haven and endeavoring to make up for never attending so much as kindergarten. I was understandably, discomfited by these unexpected guests, losing my train of thought, my faculty of speech and on one memorable occasion, almost a digit. The children, on the other hand, barely noticed our new additions to the second year pupils, continuing their work without a glance or flinch, their eyes flowing right over the living creatures suddenly sharing a bench with them, unless one was peckish enough to make the effort of catching air-borne grasshoppers worth it.

When I entered Ugandan homes, whether as a guest or an interviewer, I met with the same approach. Living creatures roamed freely in and around the houses, making their respective sounds and answering nature's call wherever it took them. These were animals I'd seen before—but I'd never experienced this sort of proximity to them. No live cow had ever entered my abode.

I was shocked at the beginning. The first time seeing a squealing pig tied to the back of a motorcycle for transport to the market is disconcerting for anyone. With time, however, I learned to appreciate that aspect of the culture. People were far more in touch with animals and Nature than the circles I am accustomed to. Humans, here, took their part in the animal kingdom, not enclosing themselves away from it all with stainless steel girders. Perhaps we, too, can learn the importance of being "versed in country things", in the words of Robert Frost— though maybe we can draw the line at dung on our linoleum.

The Unjustly Unloved Bat

I HAVE ALWAYS FELT that bats were unlovely, somewhat sinister creatures. That feeling may date back to the night when we woke up and heard something flying around our bedroom. It turned out to be a bat that had clearly lost its way. I opened a window so it could escape, but the poor thing was probably as crazed as I was, and the adventure ended badly.

As I grow more entranced by birds, I occasionally find myself at Wild Birds Unlimited, a New Jersey emporium of avian supplies. In addition to birdseed, binoculars, and guidebooks, they also offer material about bats and bat houses.

Yes, you can try to induce bats to set up housekeeping on your property. My first question was, "Why on earth would anyone want to do that?" I bought two guidebooks, hoping to be enlightened, and flipped through the pages. The gripping words "a single, little brown bat can eat from 500 to 1,000 mosquitoes in a single hour" immediately won me over.

One night, I attended a "Batstock" wildlife program in New Jersey run by Joseph D'Angeli, of NJBatman.com, who brought several caged bats with him.

After the lecture about the role of bats in the ecological system, there was a Q & A. Several fruit bats demonstrated how they eat chunks of ripe fruit from skewers thrust through the bars of their cage. They do not actually swallow solid food—after taking it into their mouths, they strain it of its juices and spit out the residue, including the seeds. These table manners enable bats to serve as important agents for seed dispersal. While birds habitually avoid large denuded areas for fear of predators, bats will traverse them, searching for food and presumably dropping seeds.

Bats also act as pollinators. They are especially important in desert areas, where they pollinate many varieties of cacti. They also pollinate many commercial crops including bananas, mangoes and guavas.

Bat-attracting flowers generally have the following characteristics: they open at night, they are large, highly fragrant, have white or pale coloration, and produce dilute, copious nectar.

Fruit farmers do not welcome bats because they suspect them of damaging crops. However, farmers are apparently not aware that fruit bats feed only on produce that is too ripe for shipment, and are, therefore, economically harmless.

Most bats fall into two categories. One type is the Old World megabats—the fruit bats—also known as flying foxes. Despite my earlier characterization of bats as unlovely, flying foxes are in fact quite cute, looking rather like inquisitive puppies. The second type is the insectivorous microbats, which have pronounced snouts and over-large ears. Some of the larger microbats will also hunt lizards, birds, and fish as well as other bats.

Echolocation—the method of locating prey based on bouncing sound waves off solid objects—a trait of microbats only, is the basis for sonar (developed by the U.S. Navy). Bats send ultrasonic waves from the larynx through the nose or open mouth and hear the return echo through their enlarged ears. Some moths have developed their own defenses against detection, but the bats are continuing to evolve their own counter-strategy.

Bats struggle, today, under serious population pressure. In addition to the usual man-made problems, they have been suffering since 2007 from white-nose syndrome, a fatal fungal infection that affects the skin, muzzle, and wings. The infection is caused by *Pseudogymnoascus destructans*; there has, however, been some recent indication that bats are beginning to develop some immunity to the pathogen. However, since most bats have only one pup a year and the population losses have been in the millions, it will take many, many years to reestablish former population levels.

If you are contemplating a bat house, let me pass on several suggestions about siting. The house should be hung on a tree trunk between fifteen and eighteen feet off the ground. It should face south-east in order to get the most sun. (Despite being mammals, bats have difficulty regulating their own temperature, so they rely on the sun as an additional source of warmth).

Under natural conditions, old trees with rotting "snags" attract bats to roost. However, in cities, we tend to quickly remove even short trunks of rotting street trees, thus preventing bats from finding new natural homes.

I have developed a new appreciation for our local bats, and I simply hope that they can keep up with the mosquitoes!

On the Road: the Good, the Bad, the Banded Snake

A FRIEND OF MINE IS A NATURE COUNSELOR at a day camp in Rockland County, New York. Last summer, thinking that having a harmless, local snake would make a great educational project for the campers, he asked the camp maintenance staff to bring him any snake that they came across.

He was expecting a garter snake. Instead, one day a staff member came running over to the nature center holding a closed bag with a snake's head poking through the top.

A quick glance revealed that this was no garter snake. Though most local snakes are harmless, one venomous type is occasionally seen in the neighborhood: the copperhead. Could they have captured one of those?

They safely transferred the mystery creature into a covered glass tank and examined it carefully. It had red, black, and white bands and was quite beautiful. A call to the local state biologist confirmed that their prize was a milk snake—a species that is safe to handle.

After a few days, they returned the banded beauty to the wild.

When I first saw the photos, I was quite taken aback. Although I do not know much about snakes, I find them extremely graceful and attractive, particularly if they are *much* smaller than I am and are not dangerous. The only banded snake of my acquaintance is the coral snake, which is not local and is, indeed, quite poisonous.

When you have little expertise, how can you quickly determine whether a banded snake you are confronting is safe or dangerous? A piece of doggerel might help. "Red touch yellow kills a fellow" pairs with "Red touch black, venom lack." Remember our milk snake features black, red, and white bands? Regardless, I treat the rare snake that I encounter with great caution.

On a recent leisurely road trip to Florida, we stopped at Devil's Millhopper Geological State Park in Gainesville, Florida. The highlight of the park is a ten-thousand-year-old sinkhole. Sinkholes are common in Florida because the underlying surface is limestone that is gradually eroding due to the action of acidic rainfall until the surface finally collapses, leaving huge craters. The sinkhole at Millhopper is 120 feet deep and 500 feet across. The vegetation covering the entire slope more closely resembles vegetation found in the Southern Appalachians (further to the north) than local Florida flora. This is probably due to the similarity of conditions inside the sinkhole to those of the Southern Appalachians: moist, fertile soil, dense shade, and flowing streams.

Florida is home to several venomous snakes. There was even a poster describing them at the park information center, and a coral snake is, of course, depicted on the poster. I was trying to show my husband how to distinguish a coral snake from its non-venomous look-alikes. As I start reciting "Red touch yellow," two voices chimed in over my shoulder with slightly different versions. One was "Red and yellow kill a fellow; red on black venom lack." It turned out that the two voices were those of local exterminators frequently called upon to deal with snakes.

In addition to the coral snake, Florida has five other venomous snakes—the Southern copperhead, the water moccasin or cottonmouth, the Eastern diamondback rattler, the canebrake rattler, and the dusky pygmy rattlesnake.

New York State has only three poisonous snakes—the timber rattlesnake, the copperhead, and the massasauga, also a type of rattlesnake. All are, fortunately, quite rare.

If you encounter a snake and are not completely clear about its identity, leave it alone. In all my years of gardening, only once did I see a snake. When digging in the soil, I tend to lift up any earthworms I have disturbed and let them go on their way. One day, I saw what appeared to be a rather long earthworm and, without thinking, picked it up. You never saw two more startled creatures! I looked at it and realized that this was no earthworm. It looked at me, remaining quite still, as if wondering what I would do next. I do not recall exactly who made the next move, but the little snake and I parted company quite rapidly.

The Bronx Zoo has a well-populated reptile house. With a strong glass barrier between me and the beautiful snakes in their collection, I can relax and enjoy the view!

What's That Black Stone?

COMBINING TWO SERIOUS INTERESTS of mine, paleontology and geology, I visited Howard R. Feldman, professor and Chairman of the Department of Geology and Environmental Sciences at Touro

College in NYC. His passions are the geology of the Mohonk, New York, area as well as the paleontology of Israel, Egypt, and Jordan, where he collects Mesozoic brachiopods. Since paleontologists—in or out of Israel—are themselves almost extinct, I was delighted to make Dr. Feldman's acquaintance.

For clarity's sake, let us first define "Mesozoic" and "brachiopods." The Mesozoic is the geologic period extending from 251 to 65.5 MYA and is itself subdivided into three shorter periods—the Triassic (251-199 MYA), the Jurassic (199-145 MYA), and the Cretaceous (145-65 MYA). Dinosaurs, to take one yardstick, began evolving in the Triassic and became extinct at the end of the Cretaceous.

Brachiopods are marine animals that superficially resemble clams. I was, however, quickly corrected. Clams are mollusks, while brachiopods are *lophophorates* because they have a specialized feeding organ called a lophophore. That being said, the easy way to tell them apart is that brachiopod shells are symmetrical through the midline, meaning that, if you slice them perpendicular to the hinge line, the halves are symmetrical to each other. Clam shells—otherwise called the "valves"—are mirror images of each other.

But I digress. While we were looking at the various treasures to be found in his workshop and study, Dr. Feldman pulled out what appeared to be a polished black stone and asked if I could identify it. He added that no one had ever done so correctly but he was willing to offer a few hints. Though I thought it would be an exercise in futility, I was willing to play Twenty Questions. The outstanding characteristic of the object was its high polish. That polish, I was told, was not the result of any geologic process such as water, wind, sand, nor was it the product of human effort.

Suddenly I remembered "gizzard stones," which some modern

animals still retain. These are stones—gravel or small rocks—that some animals swallow whole and that remain in their stomachs, where they act as grindstones to crush fibrous foodstuffs that are swallowed without significant chewing. Crocodiles, herbivorous birds, seals, and sea lions still have gizzard stones today. But how can one prove that such a prehistoric stone is similar to a present-day object?

In this case, Dr. Feldman explained that the gastrolith—from *gastro*, meaning "stomach," and *lithos*, meaning "stone"—had been found nestled within the chest cavity of a fairly complete dinosaur skeleton. Another distinguishing characteristic is that the stone must be significantly dissimilar to other rocks found in the immediate area of the excavation site. The polishing itself is also diagnostic, because the action of other gastroliths in the stomach—there can be several present at one time—and tough vegetation leaves the higher surfaces of the stone well polished, while any cavities remain rough. If you ever used a rock tumbler as a kid, you will recognize this polishing pattern.

Because I went the "Twenty Questions" route first, though, Dr. Feldman was not impressed enough to anoint me the first guest to figure it out.

Why are gastroliths necessary now, and what role did they play in the past? The question is more complicated than it sounds. Digestion is not a simple process, and animals have many different ways of extracting nutrients from their food. Hunger induces foraging and eating, and, fortunately, digestion takes place well out of sight. Many factors affect it, including what kind of food is eaten and how fibrous it is. Is the food swallowed whole or is it chewed? What kind of teeth does the animal possess?

Suffice it to say that huge herbivorous dinosaurs once existed whose teeth were not designed for chewing, only for stripping leaves off plants. The plant material would go from mouth to esophagus to gizzard, where the gastroliths would help that organ grind up the plant fibers. Stones were taken up by the animals during browsing and later eliminated either by regurgitation or fecal passage when they became too worn or too small to function effectively. The ground-up food would then empty into another digestive chamber, in which bacterial fermentation would continue the breakdown of the plant fibers into the various nutrients that could be absorbed by the intestines.

Whenever we travel, I love to collect interesting stones— but I have not found a gastrolith yet.

Close Encounters with Unexpected Animals

WHILE RIVERDALE, NEW YORK, CAN HARDLY BE COMPARED to the concrete jungle of Manhattan, continued high-density construction is making us less suburban all the time. Excluding the ubiquitous birds and squirrels and the occasional cat, mouse, and even rat, I am still amazed at the number of animal species that can be spotted here. While the deer have not yet made their way this far south, we see the occasional chipmunks, opossums, skunks, raccoons, and snakes. People have even reported coyotes, although I have never had the pleasure of meeting one. The large variety of animals is probably due to our numerous parks, particularly Riverdale Park.

The opossum presence was a real surprise. We were having company when a child, standing near a glass door and looking out onto the garden, started shouting, "An opossum! An opossum!"

I thought the child must simply have caught a glimpse of something furry, and that a fertile imagination had taken over. Much to my shock, when I looked, there was a whitish, furry animal with a smooth, rat-like tail out there—unmistakably an opossum.

I was even less prepared for the full mouth of sharp little teeth. Despite strong similarities to rodents, opossums are actually marsupials; females have a pouch in which fetal development concludes. My personal policy is never to argue with any animal in possession of sharp teeth or claws—which covers just about anything that I am likely to encounter. Despite that, I would still love to someday see that iconic image of baby opossum "joeys"—the generic term for marsupial babies—draped across the mother's back as she goes about her business.

While it is blessedly rare to see skunks here, it is not rare to smell them. As the joke goes, "Where does a skunk go when it encounters a person? Anywhere it wants!"

One evening years ago in the country, a skunk sprayed about fifty feet from our cabin. The smell was so awful that no one in the vicinity could sleep for nights afterward.

Back in Riverdale, with the advent of warmer spring weather, I began smelling skunk and even caught a glimpse of one checking out a neighbor's garden. A healthy fear continued to linger from the events of that memorable summer.

I awoke one Saturday morning with a strong smell of skunk toward the front of the house. As I walked down the driveway to collect my newspaper, the smell became stronger and stronger, until I noticed a furry mound squashed on the street. I grabbed my paper, hurried back inside, and tried to ignore the smell. That, I assure you, is impossible.

Eventually, I accepted defeat and, using disposable gloves and a heavy garbage bag, went out and bagged the corpse. Being so close to the animal, I also discovered that the two senses of smell and taste can get confused in the back of your throat when confronted by such a penetrating and obnoxious odor.

The old antidote for counteracting skunk odor is tomato juice. Having none in the house that day, I hoped that the significant ingredient in the tomato juice was the mild acid. What I did have at home was lemon juice, so I poured an entire bottle on the stain in the street in the hope that it would do the job. No such luck. Googling the situation later, I found several sites that recommended a mixture of hydrogen peroxide and baking soda, combined with a dash of dishwashing liquid.

Our garbage pickup day is Monday; I called Sanitation to see if they had any regulations covering dead skunks. They said, "No, lady. This happens all the time. Just leave it with the regular trash." My already healthy respect for the Sanitation Department went up considerably.

And would you believe, the exact thing happened several weeks later! Dealing with the cleanup yet again was no pleasure, but at least I had a routine by then and took care of it immediately. I still had not, however, laid in a supply of hydrogen peroxide!

So Many Spiny Critters

SOMETIMES IT IS DIFFICULT to be sure that you are talking about the same thing in the course of a discussion, particularly when English is not the native tongue of both parties.

Recently, in a discussion with a guest from Israel, we got onto the subject of quilled animals. The Hebrew word for porcupine is *dorban*. However, there is another Hebrew word, *kippod*, which the dictionary translates as "hedgehog." I had always assumed that the two words were interchangeable; that, like cougars and pumas, they were the same animal. It turns out that I was in error, and that we were talking about two very distinct and unrelated animals.

In all fairness, the animal I picture when I hear the word *porcupine* must *be* our porcupine, since they are New World animals occurring in both North and South America; hedgehogs, it turns out, are native to Europe, Asia, and Africa.

Porcupines are members of the order *Rodentia* (rodents), family *Erethizontidae,* and have been around since the late Oligocene (26 MYA). The etymology is based on its appearance, since *porcus* is Latin for "pig" and *spina* means "thorn." They live in woody areas, can climb trees, and give birth to a single pup, called a "porcupette," after a 16–30-week gestation, depending on species. Porcupette quills are soft. They have fuzzy red fur and can climb trees within a few days of birth. Porcupines are primarily herbivores, eating bark, conifer needles, and leaves, although some species will also eat insects and small reptiles. Because they eat the cambium (growing) layer of a tree's bark during winter, they can easily destroy trees by girdling (eating around the entire perimeter of the tree).

Clearly, the most memorable quality of a porcupine is its defensive quills, which number around 30,000. But even they are not what they seem. When a porcupine bristles and deploys its defenses, it is not actually the quills you are seeing but rather a long, thin, hair-like structure called a "guard hair." Hidden beneath these guard hairs are the four-inch quills (although quill lengths differ depending on where they are located on the body). Quills are made of keratin (a structural protein found in human hair and nails), filled with a foam-like material, are loosely embedded in the skin musculature, and are released on contact. Since they have a microscopic barb on their business end, removal can be difficult, painful, and frequently impossible for many of their predators.

Never ones to waste good raw material, Native Americans collected quills from porcupines, cleaned and dyed them, removed the tips, and used them to create decorative embroidery on clothing, moccasins, and utensils. Later, trade beads largely replaced porcupine quills for such work.

Quills can be collected from a living animal by throwing a blanket over it and then removing the embedded quills from the material. The same technique can be used today by substituting a styroform board for the blanket. The guard hairs were also collected by Native Americans and used to create roaches, a stiff, dramatic hair decoration.

Hedgehogs are an altogether different animal. They are not rodents but nocturnal members of the order *Eulipotyphla*, family *Erinaceidea*. While the fossil record is not clear, there is an early hedgehog candidate dated 125 MYA from Spain and one from British Columbia from 52 MYA (despite their total absence in the New World in the present).

The hedgehog's name is derived from Middle English, referring to its prevalence in hedges and its somewhat porcine appearance. A group of hedgehogs is known as an *array*.

Gestation time again varies with species, lasting 35–58 days, with a typical litter size of three to four babies for the larger species and five to six for the smaller ones. The babies are born with intact spines which are covered with a fluid-filled membrane to protect the mother during birth. These membranes then disappear within twenty-four hours.

Hedgehog spines, which number about 5,000, do not have barbs, are uniform in size, and are tightly embedded in the skin, so that they do not come loose when attacked by a predator. Hedgehogs protect themselves by curling into a ball by tensing a muscle along the fur–quill interface. This tensing acts as a drawstring to protect the non-barbed face, feet and belly.

Hedgehogs hibernate during cold weather. They were introduced to New Zealand in 1868 to remind the colonists of their homeland as well as help control garden pests such as slugs, snails, and grass grubs, although they also eat roots and berries. But as has happened with many introduced species, they have become pests by preying on local invertebrates and skinks (a type of lizard) as well as the eggs and chicks of ground-nesting birds. Although illegal in New York City, there are states where it is legal to keep domesticated hedgehogs as pets.

There are three other mammals with spines; let's turn to them next.

Echidnas, Spiny Rats, and Tenrecs (Ten Who?)

THERE IS ONE OTHER SPINY RODENT in addition to porcupine— the *Echimyidae* or spiny rat. Both the porcupine and the spiny rat are members of the sub-order *Hystricomorpha*, whose name comes from the Greek *hystrix* for "porcupine" and *morpha* for "shape," and which refers to certain anatomical peculiarities of the skull. While stiffness of spine varies among the different species of spiny rats, most have spiny hair on their backs and rumps.

Native to South and Central America, both rodents are herbivorous and insectivorous, and live in habitats ranging from the rat-like arboreal (tree-living) animals, to terrestrial species, to the more gopher-like fossorial (burrowing) animals. Parenthetically, I had always assumed that the word *fossil* derived from some word meaning "stone" but have come to learn that it is in fact derived from the Latin *fossilis*, meaning "dug up," and that not until the mid-sixteenth century did it come to refer to those ancient stony remains of past organisms we call fossils today.

The most unusual quilled mammal is the echidna or spiny anteater native to Australia and New Guinea. Named for Echidna, the wife of Typhon in Greek mythology, Echidna was a creature half-woman and half-snake known as "the mother of all monsters." It is a strange name choice unless you are acquainted with monotremes (which include echidnas) and their somewhat dual nature.

Specific mammalian traits include milk-producing mammary glands for nourishing the young, and hair or fur for insulating the skin, as well as sweat glands on the skin surface, warm-blooded temperature regulation, three middle-ear bones, a neocortex, and the birthing of live young.

However, mammalian monotremes lay eggs! A single egg develops over 7 to 10 days in a pouch, at which time a larvae-like creature called a "puggle" hatches. The puggle is nourished by mother's milk secreted by approximately 150 pores onto specialized hair follicles, which the puggle licks. After 45 to 55 days, as spines begin developing, the puggle is moved from the pouch to the burrow, where the mother will continue suckling it every few days. After about a year, the mother will disinvite the puggle from the burrow.

Monotremes have other interesting characteristics in which they resemble reptiles. The term "monotreme" derives from the Greek meaning ""single opening." This refers to the cloaca, a single common cavity that serves the same function as three separate structures in mammals—the genital, urinary, and excretory tracts. A cloaca is a structure common to amphibians, reptiles, and birds. Also, reptile and monotreme limbs are, essentially, attached to the side of the body, which give them a characteristic form of locomotion. Mammalian limbs are connected underneath the body.

Lastly, monotremes have electroreceptors, also more common in fish and amphibians. Receptor numbers of an echidna can range from 400 to 2,000; they're located on the tip of the snout and are used to locate prey. The platypus, the only other living monotreme, can have up to 40,000 receptors. Echidnas seem to have diverged from the platypus between 48-19 MYA, although dating is not definitive.

Echidnas are covered on the head, back, and tail by hollow, barbless quills and, when balled up defensively, strongly resemble sea urchins. Their diet consists of termites, ants, earthworms, and beetles—both larvae and adult. They require temperate temperatures and inhabit forests and woodlands. They do undergo hibernation, although they will regularly rewarm and change location in cold weather.

Finally, we come to the last group of spiny creatures, the Tenrecs. From the order *Afrosoricida* and family *Tenrecidae*, they inhabit Madagascar and parts of Africa. The subfamily *Tenrecinae*—the spiny Tenrecs— has also evolved spines and they are found only in Madagascar.

In common with echidnas, Tenrecs have a cloaca. They also have an unusually low body temperature for a mammal, ranging from 75°F. to 95°F., and they hibernate. Their spines are shorter than a porcupine's, equally distributed across the back, and do not have barbs. Although spines are present at birth, they are soft and hair-like. Like the echidna, the Tenrec rolls up into a ball to defend itself.

Some species of Tenrecs use their spines in a novel way. "Stridulation" is the term for the sound produced by rubbing certain body parts together, and that mechanism is what gives us the grasshopper's summer song. Certain Tenrecs also have such a stridulating organ, a muscle that controls a patch of differentiated spines near the rump. The sounds produced seem to be for communication regarding feeding, foraging, and other behaviors.

The Bronx Zoo has two of our five quilled animals on exhibit. A porcupine can be found in the Children's Zoo, and Tenrecs can be seen in the Madagascar exhibit.

Potpourri

Celebrating Harvests

F OR THE PAST FEW DAYS in the month of October, families have been strolling through Riverdale carrying bundles of assorted plants. While one of the plants, a date palm branch, is recognizable, the rest are more obscure. The bundle, considered as a unit, plays a role in the holiday of Sukkot, the third of the three Jewish holidays that occur in September–October, following Rosh Hashanah and Yom Kippur. One of the observances marking Sukkot involves prayers in which these plants figure.

The Torah (Leviticus 23:40), states that, during the Sukkot holiday, "You shall take the fruit of a goodly tree, palm switches, a thickened branch, and river willow bunches." The fruit of a goodly tree is interpreted as an *etrog* (citron); the palm switch, known as a *lulav* since Mishnaic times (70 CE–220 CE), comes from the date palm; the thickened branch (*hadas* in Hebrew) is a myrtle; and the river willow is our familiar weeping willow.

Dates have a long history in the Middle East, having been cultivated for over five thousand years and are native to the Southern Iraq–Western India area. They provide both an important food as well as the raw material for construction, baskets, and mat-making. Date palms are the most important tree growing in an oasis where they also provide shade for the lower-growing trees and plants. Their scientific name is *Phoenix dactylifera*. The epithet is a combination of *daktylos*, from "finger," and *fero*, meaning, "I bear." *Phoenix* derives from the ancient Phoenician word for purple-red. The scientific name is, thereby, highly appropriate because it evokes both the shape and color of the fruit.

Dates are dioecious, having tall, stately female trees which bear the fruit we enjoy while the male trees are shorter. Under natural conditions, dates are wind-pollinated, but when cultivated, they are pollinated by hand. This allows the number of fruit-bearing females to be increased at the expense of the male plants.

The *lulav* is not part of the fruiting structure of the date palm; it is simply a closed frond about three feet in length.

The *etrog*'s scientific name is *Citrus medica*. The epithet *medica* refers to the fruit's use in ancient times for a variety of medical conditions. It is one of the four original citrus fruit species from which the rest of our modern citrus varieties have been developed either through natural cross-fertilization or by plant breeding. The other three original citrus species are the pomelo (*Citrus maxima*), the mandarin (*Citrus reticulata*), and the papeda. Citrons are native to southeast Asia, though there is evidence of their presence in Luxor (Egypt) 3,000 years ago in the Temple of Karnak. Citron pollen has even been found in the plaster walls of an Israelite palace in Jerusalem dated to 538 BCE.

The myrtle is *Myrtus communis*, from the *Myrtaceae* family, related to the eucalyptus. It is an evergreen shrub native to the Mediterranean basin. The leaves are aromatic when crushed, and the plant is drought resistant. Ordinarily, this plant sprouts two leaves from a single point on the stem. But the variety used on Sukkot has three leaves instead, giving it a unique appearance.

Willows (*Salix*) are common to our area and require little discussion.

There are many theological discussions about the inclusion of these plants in Sukkot prayers. I think the explanation is straightforward. Israel, both ancient and modern, is largely arid and deeply dependent on seasonal rainfall for its existence. Our four species represent the four types of water usage by plants. The willow guzzles water and grows near running streams, the myrtle is drought-resistant, the citron is irrigated, and the date palm is found in oases where water is available from subterranean sources. Together, they represent all possible water regimes used in agriculture.

The other public Sukkot custom is the building of a small hut called a *sukkah* under the open sky (*sukkot* is the plural form in Hebrew, hence the name of the holiday). Homeowners with a yard can build one easily, while apartment dwellers usually build a larger, communal *sukkah* in the building courtyard. The *sukkahs* are decorated with paper chains and tinsel decorations that are limited only by the creativity of the owner. Since Sukkot is also known as "the Harvest Festival," many decorations are of plant origin. Multicolored Indian corn works well, as do dried flowers. The custom in my family is to hang three small bottles from the bamboo mats that serve as the roof, one filled with flour, one with oil, and one with wine, to symbolize the three basic food categories recognized in ancient times.

The Brooklyn Botanical Garden has examples of the date palm the citron, and the myrtle in the Conservatory, while they have a willow growing outdoors. If you are shy about asking a Jewish neighbor to see the four plant specimens, you can take a trip out to Brooklyn to check them out.

History of Plants in New York City

RECENTLY I ATTENDED A LECTURE at the New York Botanical Garden about Anton Kerner von Marilaun (1831–1898), an Austrian botanist and professor at the University of Vienna. Professor Kerner was interested in phytogeography, "the geographic distribution of plant species and their influence on the earth's surface," as well as phytosociology, "the scientific discipline that deals with plant communities, their composition and development, and the relationships among the species within them."

I chanced to speak with another attendee, Joel Warren Grossman, an Andean and North American archaeologist, who manages and directs excavations at challenging archaeological sites in North and South America. It turned out that he had authored the chapter "Archeological Indices on Environmental Change and Colonial Ethnobotany in 17th-Century Dutch New Amsterdam," published in the book *Environmental History of the Hudson River* (2011). The article first reconstructs the archeology and colonial history of the Dutch West India Company block in Manhattan, and then chronicles the changes in plant diversity between the seventeenth and eighteenth centuries. And to top it, off he lives in Riverdale!

Archeology is not simply dealing with far-away exotic locations whose populations have disappeared and whose buildings have been buried by jungles or sand.

By 1524, Manhattan had already been visited by the Frenchman Giovanni da Verrazzano, who explored the Atlantic Coast of North American between Florida and New Brunswick on behalf of King Francis I of France, although it was first settled by the Dutch in 1609. The famed purchase of Manhattan Island for $24.00 in beads is referenced in a letter written by Pieter Schagen on November 5, 1626. Much about that transaction remains murky, including who the actual sellers were, whether beads were really involved, and whether $24.00—instead of $1,000.00—was the actual amount of the sale. Quite a steal, regardless of how you look at it! In any case, with more than three hundred years of European-style building going on and people living in the area, there are archeological treasures waiting to be discovered buried beneath the streets of Lower Manhattan.

And so, in 1984, the New York City Landmarks Commission— established in 1965 in response to the loss of the Beaux Arts Pennsylvania Station demolished in 1963—mandated the excavation of a section of Pearl Street (originally called the Strand), which stretched along the waterfront, to a depth of eight to twelve feet. Dr. Joel W. Grossman was hired, to first develop a map-based sensitivity assessment and then an excavation strategy to expose and document the buried colonial city of New Amsterdam. His particular interests include ethno-botanical samples which would shed light on the human use of plants. The excavations covered three periods: (I) 1630–1650, culturally Dutch; (II) 1680–1700, culturally Dutch, politically English; and (III) 1710–1730+, completely English.

Using well-established archeological techniques, samples of earth were taken from twenty-six different locations where the time period could be determined. After thorough washing, 1,458 seeds identifiable down to the genus level were collected for a total of 24 groups. Of these, 19 separate genera emerged from Period I, 13 from Period II, and only 5 from Period III. The different seeds that show up in these environmental time capsules were found in various strata and building features (cisterns, wells, pits, beam slots, foundations).

According to colonial documents (c. 1633–1650 CE), the block may have included a medicinal garden belonging to Dr. Hans Kierstede (1612–1666). His wife, was the well-known herbalist Sara Roelofs (1626–1693). Sara grew up in regular contact with local Indians and spoke fluent Algonquin. She also used the Indian women as informants in matters of native medicinal remedies in the same manner as the botanists of the Dutch East and West India Companies, who routinely sought out indigenous women to learn about local medicinal plants.

Plants that are characterized as indigenous potherbs ("a plant whose leaves, stems, or flowers are cooked and eaten or used as seasoning") and starchy food sources (which may have doubled as medicinal plants) were found solely in the early seventeenth century and then disappeared. Those plants include amaranth (*Amaranthus*), lambsquarters (*Chenopodium*), knotweed (*Polygonum*), purslane (*Portulaca*), tobacco (*Nicotiana*), bedstraw (*Gallium*), and pokeweed (*Phytolacca*). Seeds of native squashes, peaches (Old World origin), strawberries, and raspberries/blackberries were also found.

Late seventeenth century evidence includes purslane, members of the cabbage family (*Brassica*—European origin), strawberry, raspberry/blackberry, peach, and cyperus (a native sedge with starchy, edible roots), and reveals a total disappearance of the native potherbs and starchy-root plants.

The early eighteenth century saw a great reduction in plant diversity. However, we suddenly see grape seeds, while continuing to see native squashes, strawberries, raspberries/blackberries, and peaches.

The establishment of cities has always caused serious habitat change even in what we consider simpler times.

The EcoFlora Project— Present (Almost) At Creation

P REVIOUSLY, I WROTE ABOUT PLANTS found in seventeenth- and eighteenth-century archaeological sites in Lower Manhattan. I want to share my excitement with you about the New York City-EcoFlora project (2016) under development by the New York Botanical Garden. In 2014, NYBG began working on a strategic plan for 2016–2021 to upgrade infrastructure, horticultural displays, plant research, and education for both children and adults.

The *EcoFlora Initiative*, inspired by two earlier studies, was presented by Dr. Brian Boom, Vice President for Conservation Strategy. The first study, known as the *Ecological Flora of the British Isles*, was proposed by E.J. Salisbury in 1928. He suggested that the collected information about British flora scattered throughout myriad journals should be systematized and located in one accessible source. That effort is now available at the University of York, which contains "data on 3,842 species of higher plants that grow in the British Isles, most native and the balance imports, that have naturalized."

The second project was conducted by Daniel Atha in a three-year study of the flora of Central Park, New York City, intended to "document and collect every naturally occurring plant in Central Park." The impressive database generated by that project can be found at the NYBG library; it contains records of 1,264 plants representing 452 species of flowering plants.

EcoFlora will attempt to emulate these projects by collecting information on all the plants growing in New York City, from the largest trees to the smallest wildflowers.

I was fortunate to meet with Dr. Brian Boom, who, together with Daniel Atha, would be leading the *EcoFlora* Project. Considering its scope and perhaps its audacity, it is clear that both careful planning and flexibility would be hallmarks of this massive initiative.

A sizable grant from the Institute of Museum and Library Services—a significant source of federal support for libraries and museums around the country— provided the seed money for developing the organizational concepts, the volunteer manpower necessary to actually collect the plants, and the framework for answering myriad questions about each plant and its ecological neighborhood .

Two terms, *phytogeography*—"the geographic distribution of plant species and their influence on the earth's surface"; and, *phytosociology*—"scientific discipline that deals with plant communities, their composition and development, and the relationships between the species within them," are at the heart of the *EcoFlora Project*.

Three planning workshops took place. The first drew on the academic community, explaining the project with an eye to recruiting volunteers for prototyping the data-collecting protocols. The second focused on environmental and government groups whose outreach and considerable local expert experience would be vital. The third focused on citizen-scientists and organizations such as *eBird* and *iNaturalist*, which were already enlisting citizen-scientists as eyes, minds, and hands in the field to expand the reach of NYBG.

The key to the success of this enormous project is the involvement of the citizen-scientist, defined as "amateur or nonprofessional scientists who forward research by their observations and collections of large amounts of data." Citizen-science is an expanding area in which the knowledgeable public collects and evaluates data in quantities that would be unthinkable for a handful of professional scientists.

Riverdale already has its own nineteenth-century citizen- scientist, well-known in botanical and ornithological circles. Eugene Pintard Bicknell (1859–1925), cited in publications as E.P. Bicknell, lived in Riverdale until 1901, at the corner of "Riverdale Lane and Old Albany Post Road" (now Riverdale Avenue).

Bicknell was a prolific collector of plant specimens, and numerous species have been named in his honor, such as *Geranium bicknelli*, which he collected in 1895 from Van Cortlandt Park, described as new-to-science by Dr. Nathaniel Lord Britton, founding Director-in-Chief of NYBG. Bicknell's collection of 12,087 specimens was donated in 1925 to NYBG. Among these, he collected the holotype—the first described and published specimen of a species—of *Sisyrinchium atlanticum* E.P. Bicknell, the colloquial name of which is Atlantic blue-eyed grass (*Iridaceae* family). His herbarium sheet can be found in the William and Lynda Steere Herbarium at NYBG.

Ecosphere Inspires

I GREW UP ON SCIENCE FICTION, whose heyday was, in my opinion, in the 1950s and 1960s. One staple of the genre was interstellar space flight by conventional rocket that would attempt a journey that could not be completed in a single lifespan. A standard solution to this conundrum was some form of hibernation or deep sleep induced in the astronauts in order to sleep through the years of the voyage without aging. My favorite solution, however, was the completely self-contained spaceship that would be its own self-sustaining world for the generations necessary to complete the journey.

In addition to needing pioneers willing to commit themselves and their descendants to the unknown for several generations, you would need a sustainable environment that would allow the passengers to be totally self-sufficient. That means they would need a way to regenerate oxygen and water, grow food, produce materials for clothing, as well as the ability to machine tools and replacement parts for their ship.

It is hard to imagine the complexity of a project of this type or the sort of people who could entertain such a vision and commit themselves and their posterity to such a voyage.

However, on September 26, 1991, eight people—four men and four women (who were not couples)—actually entered an extended structure covering 3.15 acres, partially to test out these parameters. You may even remember Biosphere 2 (our Earth being Biosphere 1), which began with a huge amount of fanfare and then largely disappeared from view by the end of their two-year stint.

I discovered, much to my surprise, that the Russians began work on this issue much earlier than the Americans did. Their enclosed environment, named Bios-3, was completed in 1972 and was intended to support up to three people in a closed system of just 412 cubic yards. Those experiments continued into the 1980s, although none of the experimental time-frames exceeded 180 days.

The Biosphere 2 experiment, which has always fascinated me, came to the forefront on a trip we made to Israel, during which we visited the Clore Science Garden, part of the well-known Weizmann Institute of Science in Rehovot. In Israel, we are always on the lookout for something educational that will excite and interest children of different ages. We struck gold with that park!

The Weizmann Institute has been ranked tenth in the world as a research facility, out of 750 institutions evaluated by the Center for Science and Technology Studies of Leiden University (Netherlands) and was the only non-U.S. institution in the top ten. It was, therefore, not surprising to see numerous installations made of simple materials designed to teach basic scientific principles in the Clore Science Park and make it look like fun. Some of their installations included a solar furnace, a parabolic listening dish, and the Archimedes Screw—used for pumping water uphill for irrigation.

You may be wondering about the connection between Bios-3,

Biosphere 2, and the Clore Garden. During a short English-language tour we ended at a geodesic dome called the Ecosphere. That was my *aha!* moment.

The Ecosphere, constructed entirely of glass panes, was designed to raise the ecological consciousness of the public. Despite not being ecologically self-sufficient, it contains land and water plants, fish, and algae. Energy for all the natural processes comes from the sunlight streaming through the building. Our tour guide, Rachel, spoke about the carnivorous plants—the Venus fly trap (*Dionaea muscipula*), the *Sarracenia*, and the sundews (genus *Drosera*). These three very different plants were used to demonstrate three different plant adaptations in response to the low mineral content of their native soil environment.

Biosphere 2 was an extremely complex experiment. In addition to the crew's living quarters there were areas designated for intensive agriculture, a tropical rain forest, a savannah, a marsh, an ocean, and a fog desert. It contained approximately 3,800 species of plants, insects, and animals. Being airtight, it had to maintain a breathable atmosphere. The Biospherians had to feed themselves and their farm animals solely from the yield of their crops, with some meat, eggs and dairy protein provided by the animals.

Several excellent books were subsequently written by individual crew members. I would particularly recommend Abigail Alling's and Mark Nelson's *Life Under Glass*.

Time Travel, Courtesy of Plants

N 1977, *SCIENTIFIC AMERICAN* PUBLISHED an article entitled "Exploring the Herbarium" by Siri von Reis Altschul. The author discussed the value of exploring herbaria as sources of new plants for use as food, medicine, and fiber. To this end, she worked at the Harvard and New York Botanical Garden(NYBG) herbaria. Despite an utter lack of interest in plants on my part at that time, the idea of solving the world's problems, with materials already collected from around the world, was deeply exciting.

In 2017, NYBG hosted an exhibition entitled *What in the World is a Herbarium?* One visitor attending the opening lectures remarked, "*I've* always wondered what exactly is in a herbarium, so I was thrilled to come today."

Opening day had two special attractions. First, the public was allowed access to the herbarium itself; secondly, they were given a short demonstration on specimen-sheet preparation, as well as the opportunity to see how the materials are digitized.

So what, then, *is* a herbarium? Think of a library, but instead of books catalogued by author or subject, imagine shelves and shelves of individual plant specimens in a temperature-controlled environment divided into 620 plant families. The storage cabinets are kept at 70° F. and 45 percent relative humidity.

NYBG has the second largest herbarium in the world, with 7.8 million specimens (the largest is at the Muséum national d'Histoire naturelle in Paris). Each year, 30,000 newly collected specimens are added to the NYBG collection in addition to other materials donated by other herbaria that have been forced to close. For example, the Brooklyn Botanical Garden's herbarium materials are now on loan to NYBG. Other acquired collections include the algal specimens from the herbarium of the Field Museum in Chicago, the Truman G. Yunker Collection of DePauw University, and the herbarium of Wabash University of Indiana, as well as personal collections such as William Mitten's collection of mosses.

The first European sheets of collected and dried specimens date from the 1500s. The concept and the relatively simple techniques needed to create them quickly spread among botanists, so that, within thirty years, it became commonplace for botanists to make and maintain their own private collections. The first herbarium, as well as the first botanical garden, was created circa 1544 by Luca Ghini—a professor of medicine and botany at the University of Pisa (Italy). At that time, there was no recognition of the fact that archival paper was necessary for mounting specimens, so botanists used whatever paper they had at hand. Unfortunately, these non-archival papers eventually break down. Sometimes the specimen can be shifted onto archival paper. When it is impossible to remove the specimen from the old sheet, a new sheet of archival quality is simply glued underneath.

One of the oldest specimens currently in the NYBG collection is a 1688 fern leaf—*Saccoloma domingense*—collected in Jamaica. As materials are reviewed, it is not surprising that new "oldest" specimens are regularly discovered.

In the field, care must be taken to dry plants quickly in order to preserve their structure and color. Care must also be taken to avoid insect infestation. Today, insect contamination is prevented by freezing the materials at -40°C. for three days after receipt at NYBG. In the past, the dangerous compound methylbromide was used. Every time a specimen is lent out and subsequently returned to NYBG, it goes through the freezing process again.

The NYBG herbarium was founded in 1891 under the directorship of Nathanial Lord Britton; its collection at that time focused on plants of the Americas. In 2002 the Herbarium was rededicated—as part of the International Plant Science Center, along with the LuEsther T. Mertz Library and Ross Lecture Hall—as the William and Lynda

Steere Herbarium.

Many famous people have contributed herbarium materials. They include Charles Darwin, Captain J. Cook, John Muir, John J. Audubon, and George Washington Carver, who, despite his fame for developing myriad uses for the peanut, was a noted mycologist.

I asked Matthew C. Pace, Assistant Curator of the William and Lynda Steere Herbarium, what he felt was the most exciting part of his job. Without a pause, he replied that working in a herbarium is "like being in a time capsule" where you are actively involved in efforts that were put into motion by botanists from many different time periods, in many different parts of the world. The herbarium is not some musty library where materials sit undisturbed forever but, instead, are part of an ongoing search for relationships between plants, between plants and the rest of the natural world, and between plants and humans. Very often specimen sheets are submitted with notations on the margins by the collector, or with journals from a collecting expedition making it feel, he said, "as if I were having a conversation with these explorers."

But what purpose does an herbarium serve?

It is important to create a baseline of all known plants. Plants, as well as animals, become extinct, and information about those lost plants is needed to fully understand climate change, the reasons for habitat loss and the activity of invasive species. In addition, plants tend to grow in communities, and understanding their interactions is vital to understanding the ecological health of an area.

Ethnobotany is the study of how indigenous people, indeed all people, use the plants in their environment as food, medicine, and material for clothing, housing, and other needs. Michael Balick of NYBG, co-founder of the Institute of Economic Botany in 1981, has studied peoples all over the world in tropical, subtropical, and desert environments. NYBG's Ina Vandebroek studies Caribbean communities in New York City. Each indigenous community contributes vast amounts of botanical knowledge about its local flora.

Life on this planet depends on plants. In order to adequately care for an increasingly densely populated world, we must have a better understanding of plant physiology and necessary growing conditions.

Modern DNA studies are elucidating evolutionary history and relationships far better than the older method of assuming that structural similarities implied relatedness. For example, the once-large lily family (*Liliaceae*)—thought to include those flowers still colloquially known as lilies as well as asparagus, onions, and agave—have been reorganized into sixteen different families.

Just as people are not identical in appearance, so too plants show some variability in the structure of their leaves and flowers. Researchers using multiple herbarium sheets of the same plant establish what are known as "type specimens." These become the yardstick for the anticipated appearance of a particular plant and, in turn, become the standard used in guidebooks and botanical illustrations.

Dating material from archeological digs can be tricky. Today, however, pollen grains, seeds, and plant vestiges are also routinely examined. Herbarium studies help identify plant remains, which aids dating as well as providing information about ancient plant usage.

Forensics also requires accurate plant data. Plant remains at a suspected crime scene can yield valuable information about the actual site of a crime as well as the season when a crime was committed.

Botanists, as previously noted, frugally used whatever paper was available to create specimen packets holding seed or plant fragments. Cultural historians can find old advertisements, ballots, and other information from printed matter on these packets to broaden their understanding of past eras.

Chemical analyses of plant fragments from bygone eras can also elucidate past environmental conditions. Studies of lead and other pollutants, as well as information about changing carbon dioxide levels in the air, are all vital bits of information allowing us to tease out a fuller understanding of the total environment of other periods.

Herbariums are an educational resource providing accurate identification of local species, information for garden clubs, samples for museums and educational exhibits, as well as conserving local materials.

If the scientific possibilities created by delving into this work excites you, volunteer opportunities exist—sometimes even from the comfort of your home. The older labels were handwritten and must be transcribed to a typed format before digitization.

If you would like to be part of this vast enterprise, check with your local herbarium.

Afterward, I began to wonder about herbariums in Israel.

With Google as my guide, I found two Israeli herbaria—one at the Hebrew University in Jerusalem, and one at Tel Aviv University. Since Jerusalem is a more convenient location for me, I e-mailed the director, Dr. Jotham Ziffer-Berger, requesting a visit. He graciously invited me, and I had a lengthy and informative visit with him and Hagar Leschner, the collections manager.

Ziffer-Berger has an eclectic educational background, but a particular interest in the bryophytes of Israel. The bryophytes include three plant groups: mosses, hornworts, and liverworts. A basic description of their characteristics includes: growing low to the ground, producing spores instead of seeds, no flowers, and no vascular (circulatory) system or only a primitive one.

Leschner had always been interested in the natural world and expected to major in zoology. When she realized that zoology research would likely cause pain to her subjects, she switched to botany.

The Hebrew University (HUJ) Herbarium was founded in 1928, and the bulk of the early plant collections were the work of early Zionist botanists. Three people of note were Otto Warburg, Alexander Eig, and Aaron Aaronsohn. Warburg, a German-Jewish botanist who did important work in industrial plantations, became chairman of the Botany Department at the then newly established Hebrew University. He asked Eig, a largely self-taught and quixotic figure, to join the faculty. Eig became the founder of the herbarium collections. Aaronsohn, born in Romania and educated in France, botanically mapped pre-State Israel. The Botany Department has since been rolled into the Department of Evolution, Behavior and Ecology.

Today the herbarium boasts between 1 and 1.2 million specimens and continues to grow as new plants are submitted, primarily by amateur botanists.

Personnel from HUJ collaborate with botanical experts from all over the Middle East. They work closely with botanists from Egypt, Tunisia, Morocco, Lebanon, and the Palestinian Authority, and routinely publish articles jointly. They have also been deeply involved with the Royal Botanical Garden in Jordan, which is under the patronage of Queen Rania, wife of King Abdullah.

"What," I asked, "is the most exciting herbarium sheet in the collection?" With a broad smile on her face, Leschner walked briskly to a collection drawer and showed me some desiccated greenish 7-to-12-inch stalks. Frequently, the dried version of common plants appear significantly different from the natural state due to changes in color, texture, and tissue thickness. So the fact that I did not have a clue to what I was looking at was not a great surprise, but it left me unable to appreciate the cause of her enthusiasm!

It turns out that the stem I was looking at came from a 6,000-year-old burial cave in Wadi el-Makkukh, in the Judean desert, 2 miles northwest of modern Jericho.

In Israel, as well as all over the Middle East, archeological remains can be found everywhere. Excavations for construction are routinely halted when artifacts are exposed. These remains, including pottery, coins, and textile fragments, require evaluation by an archaeologist before work is allowed to continue. If the find seems significant, work may be halted indefinitely.

The specimen I was shown was a fragment of burial material found in an almost inaccessible cave woven from phragmites (Family *Poaceae*), a type of reed found in wetlands throughout temperate and tropical wetlands. You have undoubtedly seen them growing around lake edges in your own area where they can be invasive.

The burial at Wadi el-Makkukh was that of a 5'6" man who had reached the then-advanced age of 45–50 years of age. He was wearing a linen kilt and sash as well as leather sandals, then wrapped in a linen shroud. The grave goods included a bow, arrows, a flint knife, a walking stick, a straw basket, and a wooden bowl. The phragmites specimen came from a woven mat upon which the grave goods had been laid.

The materials from this site, known as the Cave of the Warrior, were on exhibit in 2003 at the Israel Museum. However, once the show closed, all the materials went into storage and can no longer be viewed by the public.

My final question to Leschner was, "What is the most scientifically important specimen in the herbarium?"

That took us quickly to another herbarium sheet, which had a grassy-looking specimen.

But first we must digress. Today's plant food supply tends to depend on a limited number of major crops. The danger is obvious. When a new disease or pest attacks a particular crop, it can destroy massive amounts of vital foodstuffs quickly, with deadly results. This dependence on a single crop caused the Irish Potato Famine (1845–1852), when potato tubers, infested with the mold *Phytophthora infestans*, rotted in the fields, causing a million deaths from starvation and forcing another million people to emigrate, all out of a total population of 8 million.

Somewhat later, and first reported in 1868, the French wine industry was decimated by the destruction of French grapevines in what became known as the Great French Wine Blight. In this case the damage was caused by an aphid, *Daktulosphaira vitifoliae* otherwise known as the grape *phylloxera*, an American insect against which American vines had developed resistance; French vines, however, were defenseless. The eventual solution was to graft French vines onto American rootstocks.

More contemporaneous, and therefore more cause for current concern, has been the sudden reappearance of fungal wheat rust diseases. While fungicides can protect plants, large outbreaks could threaten the billion people who depend on wheat as a major foodstuff. First observed in 2016 in Sicily, it is being closely monitored by various governmental agencies.

This digression brings us back to that particularly important herbarium sheet at HUJ. From the above three cases of significant crop failure, it is clearly important to have measures in place to protect the world's food supply. To this end, there is an important scientific effort to maintain seed banks with multiple versions of seed—different species of the same genus—from important crop plants.

Our last case of wheat rusts highlights the need for resistant varieties of vital food crops. One scientific method used to strengthen our present crops against diseases and pests relies on reincorporating protective genes from more distant ancestors by cross-breeding.

But what is the ancestor of modern wheat? Emmer, an ancient version of wheat, has been found at Neolithic sites from 17,000 BCE although it is not known whether those samples were cultivated or foraged from the wild. But emmer wheat *was* certainly being cultivated ten thousand years ago in the Middle East and Mesopotamia.

This emmer variety, *Triticum dicoccum*, a specimen collected by Aaron Aaronsohn in 1906, was there, right in front of me! It caused a sensation at the time. And, yes, that strain is resistant to known wheat rusts!

This discovery made Aaronsohn world-famous and, as a result of a fund-raising trip to the United States, he was able to create a research station in Atlit in 1909, supported in part by the USDA, where he built up a large collection of geological and botanical specimens as well as an important library.

Like all discoveries, there are many layers to the discovery of the emmer specimen. Karl Georg Theodor Kotschy (1813–1866) was an Austrian botanist and explorer. In 1855, he went on a botanical tour of Egypt, Lebanon, and pre-State Israel, where he was collecting specimens for the University of Vienna. At that time, he collected some wild specimens of barley in the vicinity of Mount Hermon. Among his barley grains there were also a few grains of emmer wheat.

Friedrich August Koernicke (1828–1908) was a German agronomist whose particular interest was cereal grains, especially wheat. He sent Aaron Aaronsohn back to Kotschy's collection sites to collect further emmer specimens. Aaronsohn then found samples in two locations—near Mount Hermon and also in Rosh Pina, a town in the upper Galilee. Molecular studies have supported the contention that emmer is the "mother of wheat."

Aaronsohn, however, was involved in other important work. During World War I, he was an organizer of *Nili*, a group of Jews in Pre-State Israel who spied for the British against the ruling Ottoman Turks. After the war he entered politics and died under mysterious circumstances when his plane crashed over the English Channel in May 1919.

Leschner pulled out one more sheet containing a specimen of *Noeae mucronata*, or thorny saltwort. The sheet seemed less interesting than the collector, Tuvia Kushnir. He was a well-known botanist and collector with two flowers named for him, an iris named *Iris tuvia* and a desert crocus called *Colchicum tuviae*. Sixty years ago Kushnir also described the Galilee fumitory—*Fumaria thuretii*—which was only seen again in April 2017. Kushnir was killed during the Israel War of Independence as a member of the legendary Lamed Hey (The Thirty-Five).

Who knew that herbariums would be so exciting!

Hydroponics in Israel

WHY WOULD ANYONE STAYING in Jerusalem be on the roof of Dizengoff Center in Tel Aviv at 9:00 a.m. on a Friday morning, which is an hour's drive away?

The saving grace in this case is that Fridays in Israel are no longer a regular workday because, with the Sabbath (Shabbos) beginning at sundown, the workday becomes highly variable, so most offices are closed on Friday. Therefore, in Israel, Friday is a quasi-Sunday.

The important subtext here is that traffic between these two major cities is relatively light on Fridays, and the bumper-to-bumper traffic for which Tel Aviv is infamous is likewise not much of a problem then.

This adventure began several months ago when a friend, knowing of my interest in all things botanical, sent me a link about a *green* project in the heart of Tel Aviv's congested urban center. Since it concerned hydroponic gardening—gardening in water without benefit of soil—I knew I had to make time for it. Fortunately, the workshop that day was the first ever in English.

Upon arrival we found twenty people already assembled. Some were Israelis, but many were tourists. One young man from Southeast Asia, excited by the possibilities of this method, was already making plans for establishing his own hydroponics farm in his home country.

Three different types of installation were demonstrated, all of which could fit onto a small patio in the summertime or a sunny Florida room in the winter. In addition, each system could be scaled-up for a working farm. With public interest invested in organic produce combined with the pleasure of growing plants quickly from seedling to plate, this project is a win-win for everyone.

Simplicity and *low-tech* were the watchwords here as *Living Green* reaches out to the ecologically minded consumer. As Mendi Falk demonstrated the three systems currently available—a water-filled growing table, a plastic pipe system, and a tufa-based system—he kept emphasizing that the designs had been specifically created for people who lack a technical background and might otherwise be put off by complicated assembly or maintenance.

The simplest system was a ten-by-twenty-foot waterproof table with a sunken center resembling an enlarged version of a kindergarten's water-play station. The sides of the table were eleven inches high, filled with water to a depth of eight inches. The surface of the water was covered with a sheet of heavy plastic with 150 holes punched into it. Each hole was filled with a cone containing its own mature Romaine lettuce plant.

The second system, constructed out of plastic pipes with strategically placed openings was, essentially, a vertical version of the water table system. Its output is twice that of the water table unit.

The third system used tufa, a porous volcanic rock broken into gravel-sized pieces, as a growing substrate. This was set in a tabletop similar to the first system with the water table, but the growing area was filled with tufa. The water, which partially filled the tufa-filled growing area, was provided by a connection flowing through a fish tank, thereby adding fertilizer in the form of fish waste. This last system produced the greatest yield.

The two significant advantages of these systems are low water consumption (approximately one-fifth of a standard farm's usage), and the ability to grow plants where there is literally no arable soil or local water sources.

These are ideas whose time has clearly come. The *Times* recently ran an article highlighting the difficulties of finding quality, fresh produce in Alaska, where winters are not only very cold but the winter months have little or no sunlight. Two companies there are already up and running, growing local produce in the wintertime. One uses a hydroponics method related to the workshop techniques already described. The second uses a more traditional concept but does the growing in insulated shipping cargo spaces using indoor grow lights.

And yes, at the hydroponics workshop, they had a nine-inch square plastic unit that I could buy to take home and try out for myself this winter. Since it is too late in the season to buy lettuce seedlings, I'll have to germinate my own.

I cannot wait to have my own organic Romaine lettuce for our table during the winter!

Invasives

D ID YOU KNOW THAT AN APPLE can cost you $50.00 at the airport? No? It's not because the vendors there know they have a captive market. That fee had already been levied years ago on a young couple of our acquaintance who were arriving at JFK from overseas. Unwittingly, they had a miscreant apple in their hand luggage, and when asked if they had any fresh fruits or vegetables, they answered in the negative because the apple was such a negligible item that they had forgotten about it. But the apple was discovered, and they were hit with the fine.

I was reminded of this story when we ourselves landed at JFK. Passport control went smoothly. Baggage collection went smoothly and quickly. But it was turmoil at Customs. The Customs officers were checking more suitcases than in the past, and they are particularly on the lookout for any plant seeds, anything containing foreign soil or fresh meat, as well as fresh fruits and vegetables.

Years ago, when the Mediterranean fruit fly was discovered in California, we were vacationing in the western U.S. and driving a rented RV camper. As we approached the California border, there were large signs along the road declaring that every vehicle entering California would need to be inspected for the presence of certain types of fresh produce. The details escape me now, but the wait was a long one, and we had to throw out several items before we were allowed to enter that state.

All this may seem like overkill to those divorced from the agricultural sector. But a friend told me what amounts to a botanical horror story. He had been overseas, and, inveterate seed collector that he was, he had picked up some acorns that were quite different in shape from our local types. The acorns ended up forgotten in his jacket pocket. He returned to the U.S. and, one day, months later, when the weather was appropriate for a lightweight jacket, he put that one on and went outdoors. Later, sticking his hand in a pocket, he felt something hard and, pulling it out, instantly recognized the foreign acorn. Since it was already in his possession in the U.S., he tossed it into an indoor flower pot to see if it would germinate.

Imagine his horror a few days later when he found the pot swarming with tiny larvae! With great presence of mind, he took the pot and everything growing in it to an outdoor patio, and incinerated everything. But it was an accident that might have led to terrible consequences.

That brings us to serious consideration of invasive plants and the terrible damage they can cause. Personally, I have learned to rue the appearance of two plants that made their way into my garden. I initially greeted them with pleasure but realized later that they were problems. They were the Jerusalem artichoke (*Helianthus tuberosus*), which looks like a sunflower variant, and the lesser celadine (*Ficaria verna*).

Several years back, I had noticed that there was a sunflower-like plant growing sporadically along the Saw Mill River Parkway (NY). Somehow I ended up with a few seeds and waited, excitedly, for them to show me what they could do.

The first year, I had a large stand of flowers on long but weak stems. Since the stalks were thin, the plants simply fell over and created an unattractive mess that suffocated everything around them. The second year was worse. I finally decided that it was not a plant for me and, in the third year, started pulling the sprouting stalks out of the ground as soon as I spotted them. We are now into the third year of weeding them out, and I still have plants coming up despite having been careful to pull them out by their tuberous roots.

But nothing compares to the lesser celadine, a spring ephemeral. Years ago, again driving down the Saw Mill Parkway, I had spotted beautiful, tiny yellow flowers surrounded by rounded deep-green leaves and wondered how I could get some. I have no idea how they showed up one spring in a small area of my garden. Again I was thrilled. However, that small area has grown considerably over the years until the plant is now everywhere, overgrowing many of my other perennials.

I garden purely for pleasure. But just multiply these troubling, invasive plants on a commercial scale and you can begin to see the terrible ramifications.

Invisible Work: New York's Newest Garbage Transfer Station

WHEN I WAS A KID, I USED TO WONDER where all the garbage and wastewater went. The unsatisfying answers I received included things like "Nature will take care of it" or "There's an infinite supply of resources," which I found unconvincing.

Sadly, I was more on target than any child could imagine.

Like everyone else, I receive e-mails from a multitude of institutions, most of which I could do without. Every now and then I receive a newsletter from New York City's Department of Sanitation and find the occasional useful tidbit inside. That's how I found myself on a complicated subway trip to Brooklyn at 8:15 a.m., heading for a tour of the soon-to-be-opened Hamilton Avenue Transfer Station. So many people responded to the announcement that, despite adding a second tour, ticket recipients were chosen by lottery. Lucky me, I won a spot!

The new facility has four watchwords: safety, efficiency, cleanliness, and concern about possible impacts on the community. Sanitation, at the new facility, will be working 24/6, with Sundays off. However, should the Sanitation routine be disrupted by emergencies such as snow removal, it will operate 24/7.

The tour took us through the facility as if we were following a loaded garbage truck. This had us walking up a ramp overlooking the dumping floor. Each truck, identified by a unique code, enters through a mechanical door that closes immediately, in order to reduce odor leakage.

Envision a large, empty warehouse with concrete floors, built on two levels. The upper floor goes only so far, extending like a balcony over the lower floor. Each of the six trucks that can be accommodated simultaneously backs up to the low wall that separates the unloading area on the upper floor from the lower floor, allowing the garbage to fall downward onto the lower level. On the lower dumping floor, there are several front-end loaders complete with special rubber blades on the scoop's bottom edge. The blades are intended to reduce noise as the loaders sweep the garbage from the dumping floor to the shipping containers. A large control center overlooking the dumping floor supervises just this part of the process. Each eight-hour duty tour has two supervisors and twelve sanitation staff, excluding additional support staff.

Mirroring the six trucks on the upper level, on the far side of the dumping floor sit six huge metal containers into which the garbage is swept. Another machine on the floor, called the "tamper," has a long metal column that moves up and down. Its function is to keep packing the garbage into the shipping containers so that each container is completely filled with the 18–20 ton expected load. Electronic scales check the weight, so that no container is fitted with a lid until completely loaded. A separate control room oversees this part of the process.

To control odor, a huge HVAC system circulates the air inside the building twelve times per hour to remove particulates and odors before expelling the air outdoors.

Once the container is filled, it drops down another level near the barges, where it is capped with a lid. The metal lids are coded so that each container can be capped with only one specific lid. These lids are removed upon their arrival at the facility by 1,200-pound magnets. By requiring each container to be capped by only one specific lid, the system prevents inexact container closure with attendant mess and odors. Once sealed, the containers are again cleaned, in deference to the neighboring community.

After lidding, the containers are moved outside next to the pier, where a crane moves each container into a holding frame on a waiting barge. The Department of Sanitation is partnered with *Waste Management*, owner of the barges, who are responsible for the process from this point onward. This metal framework has twenty-four sections, each of which can hold two containers, one above the other. Doing the math means that each barge will ultimately hold forty-eight twenty-ton containers which is over 2 million tons of garbage each day. The daily capacity of the Transfer Station is expected to average one to one and a half barges per day.

Once filled, the barge takes its cargo to Elizabeth (NJ), and the garbage ends up in either High Acres Landfill in Rochester (NY), or at Atlantic Waste Disposal in Waverly (VA).

The Hamilton Avenue Station will service ten community board areas in Brooklyn. Riverdale's waste is processed at the Harlem River Yards and also ends up in Waverly.

Despite the unattractiveness of waste, it is hard to imagine how cities could function without sanitation services. Our health and, indeed, civilization itself depend on the invisible work performed daily by our Sanitation workers. Kudos to the men and women who make our standard of living possible!

Wild Fires

I N THE UNITED STATES we have learned to respect the destructive power of forest fires, particularly those occurring in areas suffering from drought and high winds. The loss of lives, as well as extensive property damage, is horrifying.

Our own personal experience with a mild form of wildfire—and it was scary enough—happened in Alaska about ten years ago. The forest's ecology requires a natural burn-off in relatively "cool fires" every 150 years. Because of low population density and a wetter climate, these fires are seen as relatively benign by locals, who do not fret unduly unless the fire strays too close to homes. However, it was still scary enough to send us frightened New Yorkers from Denali to Fairbanks.

Last week (fall 2016) the news reported extensive forest fires in Israel that jumped into residential areas. In the United States we have municipal fire departments in large cities, and volunteer firefighters in villages and small towns. My husband once remarked that the absence of large-scale fire-fighting options in Israel is due to the inflammable nature of construction materials, which tend to run to concrete and stone instead of the wood we use in the States. However, furniture and interior decorative elements are equally flammable.

In 2010, there was horrific fire on Mt. Carmel in Israel that consumed most of the Mediterranean forest south of Haifa. Because of the size of the blaze and the loss of life—forty-four Prison Service cadets died trying to rescue inmates—Israel appealed to the international community for help, which responded with a massive firefighting effort. At that time, the Israel Fire and Rescue Service was created to form a professional, governmental institution with 2,500 professional firefighters and 20–400 "fire scout" volunteers.

After the conclusion of the Sabbath, we checked the international news as usual and discovered that Halamish—otherwise known as Neve Tzuf—had been completely evacuated. While you may not especially remember the name of this small town, the Rosenbluhs live there. I have written about them several times in connection to the olive harvest (*Masik*) that takes place annually in their olive grove and in which we participate.

We soon learned that their house, which they had built for themselves and their growing family, was a gutted shell. All household goods and appliances had been destroyed—the books, art, furniture, photos, and family memorabilia, as well as all their clothing and linens. Since Molotov cocktails have been found in sensitive forest areas nearby, the fire was likely caused by arson and not by the usual natural conditions of desiccated plant materials, high winds, and an unfortunate lightning strike.

Because there had been fires in the area the previous day, the entire community had been put on alert by 4:00 p.m. that there might be an evacuation, and that everyone should pack a go-bag and be prepared. At 10:00 p.m. the order to evacuate came, and while fifteen homes were destroyed in the end, no one was hurt. Buses were available for those without transportation, and people were taken to, and taken in by, other communities. The Rosenbluhs, their married daughter and her family, together with a neighbor family and their six children, all ended up in the community of Alon for the remainder of the Sabbath where they were taken in. The next day, people were allowed back into Halamish to examine and protect their properties. Funds were immediately available from the government to so that people could buy essentials enabling them to manage their needs over the next few weeks.

Today, due to better understanding of the ecological impact of large-scale destructive natural events, the ultimate costs of this type of weapon should be understood as well as its impact on the land itself.

There is the obvious loss of organic material. However, there is also loss of top soil together with the release of tons of carbon and nitrogen into the atmosphere. These losses will affect future nutrient retention of the soil. Future water infiltration into the subsurface is also greatly reduced so that rapid runoff from rain and snowmelt is greatly increased and not available to thirsty plants while causing greater erosion.

Israel has been engaged in reclaiming a formerly desolate land for over a hundred years. No doubt these burned-over areas will be replanted, perhaps with an even greater understanding of what constitutes a proper balance of plants to prevent future fires or limit their damage.

However, it is pitiful to see the shortsightedness of the arsonists. It is as if one sailor on a rowboat justifies drilling a hole under his own seat on the grounds that it will only affect himself!

A Torah Garden

SELDOM DO SO MANY PARTS of my life converge at the same time: Judaism, Riverdale, Israel, and Nature. I was browsing through the *Jewish Link*, a biweekly newspaper, and came across an article on a new garden project, run by GrowTorah.org at both Salanter Akiva Riverdale (SAR) Academy and SAR High School.

Yosef Gillers and I chatted one beautiful fall morning about his vision. A graduate of Washington University in St. Louis, MO where he majored in Environmental Studies, he found his focus early on. Together with a college friend, David Fox, who combined philosophy with business smarts, they are an interesting mix of vision and talent. David, with his philosophical commitment to social justice through stewardship of the environment, created the Amir organization. Their goals are achieved by sending trained personnel to summer camps around the country to teach campers how to grow various vegetable crops, and through this modality to engage them in considering the wider issues of human needs balanced by ecological requirements. Their 2015 curriculum was "Hunger," while the 2016 curriculum was "Jewish Compassion for Animals."

Gillers, however, felt that there was a missing dimension. Having spent many years in Jewish day schools with their dual curricula—secular and religious studies—he sees the world through a wider lens. For those unfamiliar with Orthodox Judaism, it is hardly just a series of ritual activities but, instead, a "culture in a scroll"—the Torah—detailing all aspects of life, with a profound emphasis on social justice. He felt that the Amir programming should be expanded to include day school students.

Ancient Israel was an agricultural country renowned for olives, dates, pomegranates, and wine grapes. The Torah clearly mandated that the poor had rights to some of the foodstuffs grown by all farmers, in the form of certain tithings as well as taxes in-kind. GrowTorah's ethos works off these ideas.

The program was brought to the SAR schools by Reva Tokayer, a local parent who became aware of the program through Gillers' work elsewhere. Reva and Dr. Aaron Tokayer created the Neta Ilan Foundation in memory of their son, Ilan Yechezkel, who died young. The two gardens, one at each of the SAR complexes, are named "Gan Ilan"—Ilan's Garden.

Gan Ilan at the SAR Academy contains six four-by-eight-foot raised cedar beds. Last season's crops included grape tomatoes, carrots, cucumbers, and basil. Come spring, Gillers plans to add six additional beds in order to include some perennials in the mix as well as increase the area devoted to the present crops.

SAR High School has a vertical garden suspended in front of the huge front windows that stream with sunlight. This year they grew primarily salad greens and herbs. They are also starting a composting program.

While gardens need to be planted early, many crops mature after school ends. Although Gan Ilan was automated by using drip irrigation, originally developed in Israel, Gillers needed someone to step in and check on it over the summer. Along came Alex Weisberg of the Moss Café. A one-time organic farmer working in a variety of agricultural venues, he is now a Ph.D. candidate at NYU with an interest in early Judaism, ancient agricultural practices, and environmental studies. He became acquainted with Gillers at the Moss Café, where they discovered common interests. Because of his background, Weisberg was also able to offer some useful horticultural suggestions.

Presently, the program is running in four dayschools. Each receives half a day per week, which translates into four to five hours. One hour is devoted to system maintenance, the remainder to the students. During that time, Gillers is able to meet with four to six classes in blocks of forty minutes each. In addition, he is training some of the in-house teachers, so that the students can work independently. At present there is a waiting list of schools that have expressed interest.

So far, I have brought together Judaism, Riverdale, and botany. But where is the Israel strand that I mentioned at the beginning? Monotheism—The Torah—was born in Israel, and is its gift to the rest of the world. Since I was reporting from Israel when I first wrote this piece, it seemed like a natural!

Epilogue

I hope that you have enjoyed traveling with me as I have explored various subjects of interest in the natural world. We have only scratched the surface, and I look forward to continuing this journey with you in the future.

I welcome your comments and suggestions and can be reached at *greenscenesura@gmail.com*.

Index

INDEX

INDEX

About the Author

Sura Jeselsohn has been writing a weekly natural history column for the *Riverdale Press* under the by-line *Green Scene*. Initially, she worked in biomedical research labs and then switched to business. She has always been active in community affairs. Her interests include science, gardening, human dynamics, and quilting.